HEART STAYS COUNTRY

A BUR OAK BOOK

Holly Carver, series editor

Heart Stays Country

MEDITATIONS FROM THE SOUTHERN FLINT HILLS

GARY LANTZ   *University of Iowa Press, Iowa City*

University of Iowa Press, Iowa City 52242
Copyright © 2017 by the University of Iowa Press
www.uipress.uiowa.edu
Printed in the United States of America

Design by Kristina Kachele Design, llc

The University of Iowa Press is a member of Green Press Initiative
and is committed to preserving natural resources.

Printed on acid-free paper

Library of Congress Cataloging-in-Publication Data
Names: Lantz, Gary, 1947– author.
Title: Heart stays country : meditations from the southern Flint Hills / Gary Lantz.
Description: Iowa City : University of Iowa Press, 2017. | Series: Bur
Oak books | Includes bibliographical references and index.
Identifiers: LCCN 2017005976 | ISBN 978-1-60938-529-3 (pbk) | ISBN 978-1-60938-530-9 (ebk)
Subjects: LCSH: Flint Hills (Kan. and Okla.)—Description and travel. | Oklahoma—Description
and travel. | Lantz, Gary, 1947—Travel—Flint Hills (Kan. and Okla.) | Prairies—Flint Hills
(Kan. and Okla.) | Country life—Flint Hills (Kan. and Okla.) | Natural history—Flint Hills
(Kan. and Okla.) | Flint Hills (Kan. and Okla.)—History, Local. | Oklahoma—History, Local.
Classification: LCC F702.F55 L36 2017 | DDC 917.8104—dc23
LC record available at https://lccn.loc.gov/2017005976

HEART STAYS COUNTRY

According to Osage tribal historian John Joseph Mathews, a division of the tribe, the Heart Stays People, got their name from their allegiance to the earth beneath their feet—they were a group who liked to stay close to home.

I'm not Osage, but I came of age in Osage country, and the lack of wanderlust inherent in the Heart Stays People must be integral to this particular portion of prairie earth. I've spent much of my adult life living away from the place of my birth, but these rocky hills covered with grasses that wave in the wind always remain a beacon. The older I've gotten, the more I've realized that my best place remains my first place. It has taken several fits of wandering to figure this out, but in my case the adage fits—there's just no place like home.

One of my earliest memories is of being barely three years old and, when no one was watching, slipping away from our house in a little valley bordering the headwaters of Sycamore Creek. I sat down in the tall grass near an oak grove and, even though dozens of people eventually began looking for me, I didn't make a sound. I remember being absolutely happy there under a wide sky, hidden in the high grass, alone and content until an adult stumbled upon my hiding place.

Since then I've always felt most at home in my own Heart Stays place—the southern edge of the Flint Hills tallgrass prairie in

Oklahoma's Osage County, a place of grassy mounds with lots of rocks underfoot and clusters of crooked little oaks providing shade. It started young, this long-lasting love affair with a landscape that unnerves the uninitiated a little, mostly because it just seems so empty. But as a proud grasslander, I've learned over the years that the place I call home is biologically fulfilling, unique, and increasingly rare. Biologists from the National Park Service and the Nature Conservancy agree that a healthy prairie remains one of the most ecologically diverse and dynamic ecosystems on this planet—as well as one of the rarest left on earth.

Unfortunately, this landscape that once inspired rapturous exclamations from travelers heading west on horseback now mostly exists in fragments exiled from each other by cropland, cities, and interstate highways. Historically, tallgrass prairie stretched from Canada to Texas, from central Kansas to Indiana. Now the last major expanse of tallgrass occurs in the Flint Hills, a verdant landscape extending in a north–south strip across eastern Kansas into northern Oklahoma's Osage County.

I grew up learning grassland ways by helping neighboring ranchers feed cattle in winter and work calves in spring. I helped fight wildfires and listened attentively as our county extension agent lectured about native grasses, cattle, and wildlife—maybe not your typical academic agenda in most parts of the country, but perfect for those of us cloistered in a schoolhouse built from blocks of native sandstone by the Works Progress Administration during the 1930s Depression. Five of us started in the first grade and finished together in the eighth, none quite prepared for the culture shock of high school in a town that teemed with twelve hundred citizens, maybe a few more on the weekends.

After college, I went to work for Oklahoma's state wildlife agency, writing news releases and stories for the agency's monthly magazine. I learned how to photograph wildlife and how to craft stories about wild birds and animals without forsaking scientific fact. But mostly I spent as much time as possible with biologists who knew the names and habits of the creatures that lived, died, and interacted in my prairie world. I soaked up their words like some Grecian youth of old sitting at the knee of Socrates. Some of these biologists have gone on to do great things in the realm of conservation ecology, and I'm still amazed by their patience as they fielded my endless questions when I tagged along.

At Home on Prairie Earth

As the years progressed, I wrote for the Oklahoma Wildlife Federation, for a number of hook and bullet magazines, and eventually for national conservation publications I'd once regarded as near-religious texts while dreaming about publishing in those lofty pages. And whenever I could I traveled, camera and notebook in hand, from the Adirondacks to the Rockies, from the South Dakota Badlands to the Texas Gulf Coast, searching for remaining wild spots on an increasingly congested map.

But in the end the place I missed the most was where the cherty Flint Hills fade into the broad Arkansas River valley. It takes a lifetime to truly learn about a place, about its weather, plants, and animals and how all of these merge into the magic we call life on earth. And now as I near the end of my own life, I find that I'm still learning something new every day and that the land has so much to share with those who will simply remain curious, observant, and concerned.

Interest in grasslands is growing, but for many it's hard to grasp the complexity of what appears to be an unending carpet of green pressed against a huge blue sky. Prairies lack the grandeur of the Rocky Mountains or our southwestern canyon country. They're more like the oceans, a mystery you have to dive into and study. Until recently, America's picture-postcard mentality relegated grasslands to lowly status—a place to fly over in an airplane or a blurred backdrop on an interstate highway. Then Iowan John Madson, a country kid who grew up hunting and fishing along a prairie river, gave grasslands a much more flattering face in his book *Where the Sky Began: Land of the Tallgrass Prairie*. Madson's lifelong love affair with native grasslands manifested itself in prose that was as strong and rhythmic as the land itself, and people began to take notice. What they found was that our grasslands and the species that evolved with them were disappearing fast.

During the 1980s, the Sierra Club, along with other conservation agencies, pushed for the establishment of the nation's first prairie national park. The movement gained traction, then derailed due to political opposition from members of Congress who didn't feel they had much in common with the Sierra Club. It seemed the idea would die as quickly as it had taken shape until the Nature Conservancy, a group that protects land by buying it outright, decided to make grassland conservation a priority. A ranch in Oklahoma's Osage County selected by the Sierra Club to serve as a core area for its failed national park was still for sale, and the Nature Conservancy moved in quickly to buy the land and reestablish bison as the primary grazer. From these 29,000 acres purchased in 1989, the conservancy's Tallgrass Prairie Preserve has expanded to some 40,000 acres containing approximately 3,000 buffalo. As of this writing, it remains the largest parcel of protected tallgrass prairie in the nation.

Kansas joined the grassland preservation club with the establishment of the Tallgrass Prairie National Park in 1996. This too originated with the sale of a Flint Hills ranch, one near Strong City, Kansas; at nearly 11,000 acres, the setting provides a serene addition to America's national park system. But the park is relatively small by grassland ecosystem standards. As the National Park Service points out on its website, only 4 percent of America's once-vast grasslands remains to be protected. We need to protect more while some is still left.

Of that 4 percent, the two largest tracts currently under protection barely exceed 50,000 acres, and prairie wildlife needs elbow room to thrive. Lewis and Clark, as they eased their boats up the Missouri River during the Corps of Discovery, were astounded by the variety and number of wildlife species they encountered, many of which were new to science in 1804. The prairies of today, mostly vacant of all but domestic cattle, are the result of decades of indiscriminate slaughter and habitat alteration. America's flyover country, back in its wildlife heyday, was more like the African Serengeti than Old MacDonald's farm.

Prairie lovers are a passionate lot, and in prairie states like Iowa and Illinois, where row crop agriculture is king, they're working to preserve native plants in old cemeteries, hay meadows, and odd lots that have managed to survive the onslaught of the plow. Modern prairie enthusiasts have also devoted themselves to prairie restoration where it is feasible, and as the science improves so does the number of acres where big bluestem and Indiangrass now thrive in place of nonnative fescues and bromes.

Like all grasslanders, I love late summer when tall bluestems bend and dance with the wind. But I also realize that if we're to preserve more than just symbolic grass farms, protected prairies must be big enough, and their location to other protected grasslands near enough, to allow for biological interaction on an ecosystem scale. Birds and animals that evolved to mingle on millions of acres simply aren't genetically programmed to survive when habitat shrinks to a few thousand acres here and a few hundred acres there. That's not much different from expecting wildlife accustomed to endless open vistas and unrestricted movement to find happiness and long-term health in a zoo.

With bison back in place as the keystone species, wildlife managers can begin the process of real prairie restoration at an ecosystem level. The grassland itself is only the canvas—add buffalo, birds, butterflies, and the other endemics that now survive on the cusp of extinction and suddenly what was once just flyover country is crammed with tourists, cameras in hand. I've seen it happen at the Nature Conservancy's Tallgrass Prairie Preserve, where the lonely dirt roads of pre-preserve days are now dusty with automobiles driving ten miles an hour with the windows rolled down, their occupants hoping for a glimpse of a buffalo. And I'll never forget a winter's day in northeastern New Mexico, when drivers pulled off the highway to gawk at a scene that would have fit comfortably in the movie *Dances with Wolves*. Hundreds of buffalo chomped on yellow grama grass, the shaggy animals ringed by dozens of beige and white antelope, while half a dozen or more coyotes circled this mass of browsers and grazers, hoping that somewhere among all those hooves they might spot a morsel of food. Media mogul and buffalo rancher Ted Turner had managed to turn back the clock by creating a living mural, made even more complete with prairie dogs, swift foxes, and burrowing owls, the animals altogether presenting a scene missing since Santa Fe Trail days.

Not long ago, I learned of another prime piece of southern Flint Hills prairie to receive protection. It contains 43,000 acres and includes the headwaters of Sycamore and Hominy Creeks mentioned in the essays that follow. This ranch is only a short drive from the Tallgrass Prairie Preserve, the Western Wall unit of the Oklahoma wildlife department's Osage Wildlife Management Area, and the U.S. Army Corps of Engineers' public use areas on Kaw and Hulah Lakes, federal land offering access to Birch Creek and the Arkansas and Caney Rivers. These public lands aren't adjacent or overly large, but for prairie plants and wildlife they offer more of a refuge than you'll find in most of the original prairie states.

The musings contained within this book originated from notes and photographs taken at the aforementioned places or on nearby private land over a period of more than thirty years. Some of the thoughts reach farther back to when my family lived in a ramshackle house near the spring that fed the headwaters of Sycamore Creek. I've remained close to this particular patch of oak trees and grass for nearly seventy years, and it hasn't changed much—some of the oil field scars have healed, new ones have taken their place, the prairie-chickens are gone, but white-tailed deer and wild turkey have returned. My hope is that hundreds of years from now it will still be much the same as when I left it and that the grass will still grow tall, cattle or buffalo will still grow fat, the springs will still flow fresh and clean. Come to think of it, considering how much we've taken from this forgiving old planet, that's not really too much to ask.

It was the same every morning. I'd listen for a man on horseback, wailing like some wild animal in distress. For months he was part of the winter landscape, a ritual of motion, a mantra steeped in supple horseflesh and bawling cattle. The high-pitched summons began in autumn, after the native grasses grew dormant and the cowboy began feeding cottonseed meal, or "cake," in pellets the size of a grown man's big toe. They'd nurture the hundreds of Hereford cattle wintering in the pasture where we lived. Not long after sunup, the cowboy would ride past our house on a big sorrel quarter horse, a lanky animal with a long head, a white stripe from forehead to tip of nose, and a contrasting red-brown coat and mane. This lean man with his weather-creased face followed a trace of dirt road west, riding at a fast trot, dressed in jeans, brown canvas work jacket, lace-up work boots, and a billed cap pulled down tightly to keep it from blowing away. And as his long-legged horse jogged along, the cowboy would issue a wild and wordless lament, his cattle call.

It was our morning anthem, a signal to begin the half-mile trek over the hill to the school bus stop. Soon the cattle came galloping into sight, moaning and grousing in cow talk, each the same reddish brown as the cowboy's horse, all with white faces, all galloping to the little green shed where sacks of feed were stored. The cowboy would cut open the hundred-pound bags and fill long sheet metal troughs. The cows would jostle each other, crowding to line up for breakfast. Later they would drift away to graze, loaf, and go about the business of being cows. The cowboy would ride back to his ranch house beyond the hill, and quiet would spread over the little valley where the headwaters of Sycamore Creek trickled from a small spring.

When the weather warmed, generally in early April, the grasses broke dormancy and sent up new green shoots among the parched tan clumps of the previous summer's growth. At that time the cowboy's morning ritual would end, to be resumed in late October or early November. Until then the cattle would fatten on the native and nutritious prairie bluestems, Indiangrass, and switchgrass. Oftentimes in early spring, a smoky haze hung over the rolling prairie as ranchers set fire to old, dry grass stalks to hasten new growth. Spring thunderstorms added to the swelling greenery underfoot. By May, the rolling topography of the prairie was as verdant as any Irish dell.

Ours was a grassland economy in a land tailored for cattle and grazing. The Flint Hills, the most extensive stretch of tallgrass prairie left in the United States, reach from near the northern Kansas border south into Osage County, Oklahoma, where I grew up. These hills contain a mostly unbroken strip of native grassland more than two hundred miles long and nearly eighty miles wide in places. It's a landscape of rolling topography, where outcropping limestone and shallow soils have preserved original prairie plants, protected them from the plow, and allowed this to remain some of the best grazing land in the world.

My childhood home lies at the southern extreme of the Flint Hills, less than fifty miles south of the Kansas state line near the Oklahoma town of Pawhuska. Pawhuska, named for an Osage Indian chief, is the Osage County seat and the tribal headquarters of the Osage Nation. Although geologically and botanically the same as grassland north of the Kansas line, this southern extension of Flint Hills grazing land came to be known as the Osage Hills or, simply, the Osage, because the country was, prior to Oklahoma statehood, the tribe's final reservation. To the south, the prairie fades into the timbered Arkansas River bottoms. To the east, it eases into patches of dense Cross Timbers woodland, an ancient, scrubby forest of mostly blackjack and post oaks. To the west, the prairie begins to climb, level out, and lose its rocky substrate. Soon the land becomes a tidy checkerboard of industrial agriculture, mostly fields of winter wheat.

These wheat fields are planted annually. The perennial grasses on the prairie renew themselves from rootstock, regenerating for decades before they die. They're nourished by rain that falls mostly during the growing season and averages thirty-five inches or more a year, although periodic drought can lower that figure dramatically. Pruning by livestock and fires combine to keep encroachment by woody plants at a minimum. It's a simple system, providing a means of feeding people that in many ways reflects practices that predate recorded history.

Grazing cattle on native grass offers a workable and generally profitable way to make a living, due to the remarkable carrying capacity of healthy grassland. The key can be found in the evolution of an ungulate's gut, adaptations allowing a cow to convert tough plant material into meat. Ranchers simply apply a match now and then to stimulate the renewal of succulent green pastures. Then they watch and wait while rain, sunlight, and fertile soils cook up a bovine smorgasbord.

Precise figures don't exist, but some of today's environmentalists speculate that tallgrass prairie was, prior to Columbus, common in fourteen states and once covered around 40 percent of the United States. Today much of this former prairieland grows corn. For example, Iowa, a former prairie state, has been so thoroughly converted to row crop agriculture that the majority of the state's native grasslands are now under cultivation. Flint Hills native grass was spared conversion to cropland by thick layers of sedimentary rock that outcrop across the terrain or lie just under the surface of the soil. You'll find some arable land in the stream bottoms, but not much. The rocky nature of the landscape forced farmers to look for homesteads farther west, where they found level, deeper soils that didn't dull a plow. Ranchers, however, quick to learn that the bluestem pastures of the Flint Hills fattened a steer at a profitable rate, were lining up to lease grazing land from the Osage Indians as early as the 1870s.

Ranchers and Indians proved to be environmentally compatible prairie hosts and remained so until the early 1900s, when oil production in the southern Flint Hills began to flourish and both landscape and lifestyles experienced changes. Oil leases were a boon to some northern Flint Hills ranchers, who used the royalties to improve their holdings or to hang on financially when drought parched the generally verdant landscape. Down south in the Osage country, however, royalties were reserved for members of the tribe. As a result, royalty payments from an oil boom peaking in the 1920s generated fantastic wealth for Osage tribal members, who soon found themselves among the richest people, per capita, in the world at the time.

Today oil production is waning here in the southern end of the Flint Hills. Towns are dying, schools are consolidating, and overall population numbers are shrinking as the region returns to mostly cowboys and Indians as the petroleum industry fades. Fortunately, the people who remain are still culturally connected to the landscape underfoot, a fact underscored by the region's resistance to lifestyle changes that might undermine the ageless rhythms of cattle fattening on native grass.

Environmental leaders like the Nature Conservancy claim that grasslands are the most endangered of our ecosystems, and worldwide they struggle to gain protection. Mountains, seashores, and rain forests tend to excite the public's imagination while grasslands, ranking among the most biologically complex ecotypes, seem bland at first glance. Prairies support myriad life forms, from birds to plants to reptiles and amphibians. Today a sobering number of these grassland species are disappearing at an alarming rate as their support system disintegrates into ranchettes, energy development, urban sprawl, or agribusiness. America's tallgrass prairie, as unique as it is, could easily become biologically bankrupt if the remaining acreage shrinks much beyond what remains.

Fortunately, an ageless agricultural symbiosis of herder, cow, and grass, aided by an unyielding understory of rock, has kept the Flint Hills, America's only remaining tallgrass prairie of any significant size, in a nearly natural state. In doing so these hills continue to provide a refuge for unique yet declining species, from frog to grassland grouse to snake to butterfly. In the following essays, you'll be introduced to some of these rare plants and animals. Each entry is drawn from a lifetime of observing and the field notes that happened as a result. In writing these, I can only hope that my love for the tallgrass country will be passed along to others, people who may someday also be inspired to help protect what's left.

Hominy Creek is about seventy-six miles long, with headwaters rising in the rolling prairie of Oklahoma's Osage County. During the initial one-third of its journey to merge with Bird Creek, the Verdigris River, and eventually the Arkansas River, this small stream descends through bluestem cattle country and scattered patches of oak-hickory forest. After leaving the high prairie, Hominy Creek settles into flood-prone lowlands and tall timber, where it grows murkily more sullen and southern.

At its tallgrass upper end, Hominy Creek is a classically pretty prairie stream, despite the corruption of its name by Anglos who couldn't twist their tongues around the Osage language. In Osage, Hominy Creek is actually Walks in the Night Creek, named for Ho'n-Mo'n-I'n, a warrior held in high esteem for his exploits in battle. Walks in the Night Creek is, in the Osage tongue, Ho'n-Mo'n-I'n Ga-Xa. It's one of several small streams draining mostly native grassland in this part of the southern tallgrass and receives, on average, anywhere from thirty-six inches of annual rainfall at the headwaters to forty inches or more before emptying into Bird Creek.

Average temperatures around the headwaters of Hominy Creek range from a high of 93 degrees in July to a low of 23 degrees in January. Average wind speed is nine miles per hour, humidity ranges from around 40 to as much as 94 percent, and the average growing season runs from about April 5 to approximately October 30.

Snowfall is generally rare, with anywhere from an inch to sometimes as many as ten inches falling from late November through early March. The severe weather season can start in late March and last through May; tornadoes are a fact of life, as are violent thunderstorms with hail that may be as small as peas or as big as softballs.

Summers are hot, winters are short yet cold, and the transition periods are unpredictable. In fact, the headwaters of Hominy Creek can host some of the most erratic weather in the continental United States, according to meteorologists who come to Oklahoma to study such things. For some residents of short duration, the tempestuous weather is nerve fraying, and they go elsewhere. For the others, the rapidly changing skies are an antidote to boredom, and they'd live nowhere else.

On this particular March 16, Hominy Creek is running clear and fast through a series of upstream stony riffles, as the landscape around it continues to awaken in the days prior to the spring equinox. A quickly passing shadow warns of a flyover by a mature bald eagle, the glistening dark brown and white bird soaring low over the spot where water from a bedrock pool spills over a ten-foot-high sandstone ledge. A rust-colored fox squirrel spots the keen-eyed predator and quickly circles around the trunk of a large post oak, placing some sixteen inches of tough hardwood between it and a raptor hungrily in search of breakfast. Below the tree and several tiers of outcropping limestone, a chorus of leopard frogs commences with a cacophony of grunts, snores, and rattling trills that sound almost swinelike and aren't the least bit musical.

One of the frogs leaps into a thick mulch of pale brown oak leaves lining the stream bank, and I'm able to see the dark brown blotches on a tan background that enable the amphibian to blend nicely with the bland setting. Yellowish dorsal lines have a slight break near the hind legs, indicating a plains leopard frog, *Lithobates blairi*, named for Frank Blair, a Texas zoologist. Albert Blair, Frank's brother, was a member of the faculty at the University of Tulsa from 1947 until the late 1970s and a consummate naturalist. Even after a heart attack slowed him, Albert Blair spent as much time afield as possible, sometimes probing the springs and waterfalls along upper Hominy Creek. Although more than thirty years have passed, I can still see him snagging a diamondback water snake by hand, all the while dodging the anal excretions the snake was emitting in copious amounts in an attempt to persuade its captor to free the vile-smelling reptile.

On that day we collected tiger salamanders from a pool in a small spring-fed stream spilling into Hominy Creek, plus some hybrid oak acorns the crusty old professor would present to a botanist colleague back at the university. We also examined flowering pawpaw bushes growing along the banks of Hominy Creek and debated whether they were a natural western extension of plants more commonly found in the Ozark Mountains or, as some researchers contended, the offspring of plants grown from seeds carried west and planted by Indians.

Pawpaw fruits are, like serviceberries, hard to come by in the wild due to the number of critters that like to eat them. Yet they transplant well, and I've grown pawpaws from seeds as far west as central Oklahoma. Here in the narrow valley of Hominy Creek they survive quite nicely, along with other species more common to the Ozarks. Jack in the pulpit and Dutchman's breeches can be found growing along the shaded stream, while bladdernut, a shrub with lovely dangling white flowers, graces damp limestone terraces along with resurrection and walking ferns. The valley is deep and damp enough to allow these plants to survive periodic drought and the desiccating summer winds that rake the grasslands above.

The mingling of eastern and western species along these tallgrass prairie streams makes for a rich biological broth, one in which a devoted naturalist should never tire of discovering extended ranges and hybrids. At the same time, species from the south have continued to creep northward as the climate warms, most notably the nine-banded armadillo, a proficient digger and destroyer of gardens that hasn't met with much of a welcome mat in its new northern range.

Once during our walks, I asked Professor Blair what he thought was the defining difference between ecoregions—why, for instance, while many Ozark plants followed streams west into the prairie, the varied and abundant salamanders in the western Ozarks seemed to encounter an invisible line beyond which they wouldn't colonize similar habitat. He replied that regional extremes kept species in check. While tallgrass prairie and Ozark woodlands might share similar rainfall and temperatures for a number of years in a row, sooner or later an extreme year or a series of extreme years created physiological barricades that less adaptable species couldn't cross.

In the 1950s, for example, during the second period of extreme drought in that century, jackrabbits and shortgrass prairie plants drifted east as their comfort zones shifted. At the same time, plants and animals from the eastern woodlands that had colonized suitable prairie stream valleys lost any habitat they had gained due to several years of soaring temperatures and scant rainfall. When the drought ended and temperatures moderated, the drifting began all over again.

So when we peer through a telescope and eye a distant planet with daydreams of colonization, I guess we're not much different from a salamander or an armadillo. Life is restless, always seeking a little extra elbow room. Along Hominy Creek, the difference between solar systems can be as little as a few feet of vertical space, amounting to a little less wind, a little more shade, and moisture that lingers long enough to give life a chance.

The observation blind was not much bigger than a walk-in closet, with just enough room for four. We found it after stumbling overland in the blackness of a predawn April morning. Atop a hill amid nearly feature-less high prairie, there was nothing but grass, a breeze, and the dark—no ranch house lights, no blinking oil field derricks, no microwave tow-er's monotonous flash. Then, out of all this inky space, came a low eerie sound as if prairie zephyrs were practicing ventriloquism. At times the strange crooning seemed like pigeons cooing. Yet the notes were more resonant, more liquid, more like the merging of tumbling water and rushing air.

The courting song of the male greater prairie-chicken has been described by some as the sound made by blowing across the top of a bottle. Others say it's more dovelike, but even the lamenting dirge of the mourning dove doesn't contain the wind chamber–didgeridoo effect of these wild grouse. The call notes emanate from inflatable air sacs on the cocks' necks and the results are low and soothing, like the murmuring of spring wind. The sound carries great distances across the prairie grasslands where cock birds court hens each spring. On this April morning, the pale glow of first light revealed that the cho-risters were already in place—maybe a dozen roosters, each strutting and serenading while several hens strolled the closely cropped dance grounds, studying the masculine attributes of the suitors vying for their mating favors.

The lek or booming ground used by greater prairie-chickens summons birds year after year, generation after generation. The spot is generally somewhat elevated with low, sparse ground cover, good both for prairie-chicken narcissism and for spotting potential predators planning to drop in unannounced.

This lek was near the heart of the Nature Conservancy's 39,000-plus-acre Tallgrass Prairie Preserve north of Pawhuska a few miles south of the Kansas state line. The morning was somewhat cool and the chickens supercharged with breeding ardor. At times the cocks appeared possessed by some maniacal spirit as they stamped their feet with jackhammer speed, tail feathers erect and a pair of pinnate feathers sticking straight up above each ear like devilish horns. Cupped wings were spread just enough to ensure that the tips would drag the ground as they danced. The vocals, or booming, began when each male forced air out of his throat sac, then over his vocal cords with a noticeable forward-thrusting motion. The result was the otherworldly, sonorous cooing that reverberated over the grasslands like a feathered woodwind symphony.

If a challenger invaded the invisible perimeter encircling a rival's dance space, the two would face each other beak to beak. Next the birds sprang several feet into the air, flailing away at each other with wings and spurs like a pair of domestic fighting chickens. Each leap was accompanied by loud cackling, the sound wildly witchlike compared to the soothing predawn call notes of eastern meadowlarks and mourning doves, birds whose voices were rising in volume all around us with the increasing light.

At times the cocks would even perform their drumming dance on the tin roof of the observation blind, as if pleased by the added resonance. Greater prairie-chickens, although wary of natural threats, show little fear of unnatural objects and have been known to display on the hoods of pickup trucks parked near their booming grounds.

On this particular morning, very little occurred to detract from the chickens' enthusiasm until, well after sunrise, a cruising northern harrier caused the birds to freeze in place. Just a moment before, the lek had been loud and boisterous. When the harrier came into sight, gliding silently just above the tips of the dried prairie grasses, the chickens

Dancing Up a Prairie Sunrise

suddenly seemed to disappear as they huddled tightly against a brown meadow just beginning to show streaks of new green grass. Within seconds, the hawk drifted out of sight and courting activities slowly resumed. But by this time the air was warming, and it was apparent that the birds' interest had waned.

Within thirty minutes the last of the prairie-chickens had left the lek, flying back to the more mundane business of foraging and resting until more nuptial jousting summoned the following dawn. Then the audience would consist of a coyote with new pups to feed, alerted by the wild cackling. Upland sandpipers would sit atop distant fence posts, awaiting more sunlight to illuminate their own nuptial flights. And here on the Nature Conservancy's prairie preserve, a buffalo bull might amble closer. The massive animal cared little about bird antics, but he was vitally interested in the arrival of tender spring grass. Except for an occasional predator, the size, shape, and species of those in the audience didn't generally matter to the hens. They sauntered across the booming grounds, carefully noting all this energy and activity expended on their behalf, watching closely as their suitors gyrated and sparred, boomed and cackled in a fanatic effort to solicit favorable attention. In time each hen decides upon a champion, and this dominant male is rewarded with an opportunity to pass his genes on to the next prairie-chicken generation.

Shortly after mating, the hen prepares a nest in a dry tussock of bluestem grass left from last summer's growing season. Next she lays eggs and broods her young, the male bird's role in the procreation process long since forgotten. By the following spring, the presiding cock of a year ago might be driven from the lek by a younger and more vital male ready to assume the role of ringmaster at this wild and wind-blown mating ritual. Among greater prairie-chickens, status can be fleeting and life can be short. Therefore, it just makes genetic sense to dance as if there's no tomorrow.

In 1850 S. W. Woodhouse, a naturalist-physician assigned to a government survey crew, took extensive notes on the nature and wildlife of what was then Indian Territory. Woodhouse and his crew passed near the modern town of Tulsa on their journey, then rode west along the southern edge of the Flint Hills.

Woodhouse noted that he saw "immense flocks" of upland sandpipers picking over burned patches of prairie as they searched for parched grasshoppers, birds grown exceedingly fat from all the wild bounty. His journals contain passages about great numbers of wild pigeons that nearly broke down trees with their weight and the numerous greater prairie-chickens he saw across the state, especially along the Arkansas River in autumn.

In his journals, published as *A Naturalist in Indian Territory*, Woodhouse wrote of large flocks of prairie-chickens, one flock with seventy-two birds, others with more, seen in trees along the Arkansas River in November. Woodhouse said the birds were perched in oak groves, feasting on acorns. As recently as the 1980s, encounters with prairie-chicken flocks seeking oak groves for an acorn feast were still fairly common in the countryside where I grew up.

Watching prairie-chickens and being concerned for their welfare have been an important part of my personal history. I hunted them as a kid, then worked on prairie-chicken conservation through jobs with the Oklahoma Department of Wildlife Conservation and the Oklahoma Wildlife Federation. I was in the field during the 1970s when prairie-chicken numbers in Oklahoma's Osage County were still high enough to warrant a popular hunting season. Numbers remained stable until the early 1990s, when the population began to crash in the Oklahoma portion of greater prairie-chicken range. Hunting here was discontinued in 1997. In its heyday the Oklahoma chicken season, held around the time of the first frost in late October or early November, drew thousands of hunters to small towns like Nowata west to Fairfax and Shidler in the Osage Hills. Cafés opened at four in the morning to accommodate incoming hunters from across the state, and the state wildlife department planted milo fields amid the big prairies to draw the birds within range of the gunners.

The hunts were more like a festival or a party than any sort of serious outdoor pursuit. At daybreak it appeared that a gunner could be found crouched at the base of every milo plant in every forty-acre field. The prairie-chickens were extremely fond of this domestic grain species, and the flocks came into the fields like kamikazes, undeterred by the bristling shotguns beneath them. The result was an orgy of exploding shotgun shells and an avian bloodbath.

I can remember big flocks of prairie-chickens flying from the high prairies around Pawhuska south to oak woods bordering the Arkansas River, much as Woodhouse described in 1850. Once in the early 1990s, following a snowstorm in late November, my father and I drove out to a patch of blackjack and post oak timber on a hill overlooking the headwaters of Hominy Creek southwest of Pawhuska. The snow, several feet deep, covered any grass and wildflower seeds. Hundreds of prairie-chickens had taken to the trees, perching on oak limbs, dining on any acorns that hadn't fallen. The sky swirled with prairie-chickens flying from one tree to another, and in typical prairie-chicken fashion the birds mostly ignored us as they went about the business of stocking up on calories. The chickens picked acorns as if they were picking ripe grapes off a vine, and it was fascinating to watch acorns roll down the birds' throats as they swallowed.

That was the last large gathering of greater prairie-chickens I would see in Oklahoma's portion of the Flint Hills. Within a few years, the countryside around this particular oak grove was totally devoid of chickens, even though it remained excellent native grassland and was well managed as far as cattle grazing was concerned.

Biologists with the Oklahoma Department of Wildlife Conservation are still speculating about the demise of greater prairie-chickens in the southern part of their range. Over the years they've mentioned disease, habitat fragmentation, woody plant encroachment, too much prescribed burning, too little prescribed burning, an increased amount of nest predation, climate change, or a mixture of some or all of the above. And while the speculation continues, a significant part of the tallgrass prairie, essentially much of the country south of the Kansas line, has lost its totem bird.

During my last visit to a greater prairie-chicken lek in the Osage Hills a few years ago, only about a dozen birds danced on a smooth half acre atop a gentle rise north of the Osage Indian village of Grayhorse. The spring booming ground here borders a gravel county road, so it was easy to simply pull over, point my camera out the window, and await the sunrise.

Within minutes a red-orange orb slipped over the edge of the earth, illuminating what remained of the previous autumn's grasses. Beyond this tallgrass border, male prairie-chickens kept up a drumroll with their feet on a lek covered with short bleached-white grasses.

As they danced, the males broke the silence with their ethereal summons. The sound carried over the grassland like the low notes of a traditional wooden flute, except this was more liquid and remained audible over an astonishing amount of space.

Lady chickens drifted in to see what all the commotion was about, and as the sun grew higher I noticed that the booming ground had been the site of another mating ritual not long before. The place where the chickens danced was littered with beer cans, and it was obvious that several cars filled with local youths had pulled over at this spot to listen to music, drink, talk loudly, posture, and strut in an attempt to impress the ladies. Without a doubt the female *Homo sapiens* along for the ride studied each male in the same manner that the prairie-chicken hens did and, perhaps to the consternation of their parents, with the same biological results.

It was sad to think that young people would trash a spot that most likely had summoned prairie-chickens to their spring rendezvous for decades, maybe centuries. Yet it was doubtful that the teens had ever

Save the Last Dance

seen a prairie-chicken, much less grasped the meaning of a lek and its implications for the future of this tallgrass prairie original.

The prairie-chicken is not a particularly adaptable bird and therefore not a strong survivor when its habitat shrinks or suffers. Judging from the grassland grouse family track record, the remaining species will not retain a presence on this planet without closely supervised assistance, especially without guaranteed space to boom, cackle, strut, and scrap, a place to endlessly practice the art of simply being a prairie bird in its original prairie world.

FERNS PRONE TO TAKE A STROLL

Among my favorite ferns are a pair found on Hominy Creek's rock walls and the automobile-size boulders that have broken away from them. The aptly named resurrection fern can appear to be as shriveled and dead as a discarded grasshopper wing when the weather is hot and dry. Then when the rains come, the fern swells back into good health and once again becomes a stout green citizen of the Hominy Creek biota.

Resurrection ferns can lose as much as 95 percent of their moisture content during drought, an amazing trait when you consider that most plants and animals can lose only from 10 to 20 percent before expiring. When the rains begin to fall, the fern quickly rehydrates and within hours resembles the healthy, robust plant it was before drought set in. An epiphyte, the resurrection fern draws nourishment from air and ambient moisture. The rocks it clings to only provide an anchor, a place to conveniently position itself while awaiting the rain.

Walking ferns are named for their ability to colonize moss-covered slabs of limestone bedrock. The species is evergreen, leathery, and shaped like an elongated spearhead stretching some twelve inches to a slender narrow tip. Walking ferns like their boulders shady and moist, and they really like the company of other walking ferns. The extended tip grows in an arch until, touching the moss it is seeking, it forms a new plant at the point of contact. A colony may consist of dozens, maybe hundreds of ferns leapfrogging and overlapping each other, forming a tapestry of bright green moss, dark green ferns, and maybe a smattering of red columbine flowers in season.

The deep leaf litter accumulating at the bottom of the bluffs bordering Hominy Creek has, by mid-March, parted to reveal the pale green leaves of white trout lily, the new growth reaching up through the moist duff like a hand protruding from a grave in some horror movie. Trout lily leaves can be pleated, mottled, and a bit fleshy, perfect for the season of the equinox. The mottling is a splotchy dark green on light green, and it matches the spotted shade of the leafless landscape. Newly emerged trout lily leaves tend to be either singles or doubles, the former still in the process of development, the latter mature enough for flowering. Basal leaves are two inches or more wide and some six inches long. A stalk bearing a single flower emerges from the paired leaves, a lovely nodding bloom consisting of six recurved sepals, six stamens with long yellow anthers, and a slender style, all artistically gathered into a vernal package an inch and a half long.

Trout lilies are pollinated by bees programmed to jump-start their annual life cycle early in the spring season. Many of these are nectar sippers, some pollen gatherers. A warm sunny day in March can literally be abuzz with bees and bee flies of various sizes and shapes, many quite tiny and reflecting sunlight in iridescent shades of blue and green. The giants among these March pollinators are the lumbering bumblebees, recently awakened from winter slumber and ready to start the process of building a new colony, a task they seem to approach with a blue-collar work ethic.

And while ground-hugging colonies of trout lilies attract their share of pollen and nectar shoppers, the busiest and loudest gathering of winged pollinators can be found buzzing around March-flowering plum thickets. The thick white flowers on these chest-high trees can be mistaken for a patch of snow against the drab brown March background. At the same time, the sweet scent of flowering wild plums is unmistakable, intoxicating, and obviously alluring.

When wild plums are flowering, the influx of insects resembles the crowd at a concert. They circle, stumble, buzz, and labor to gather some of the prairie's earliest bounty, all the while pollinating flowers that will become tasty red fruit about half the size of a golf ball by the time July heat sets in. Pollinators swarm tangled plum thickets while warm March afternoons resonate with insect voices in various pitches, ensuring that the birth of a season kicks off with an orgy that smells simply delicious.

March flowers like trout lilies can be striking yet sometimes difficult to locate as their leaves blend easily into early spring's mottled shade. Flowering plums, on the other hand, are visually flashy and aromatically appealing, the life of the season's first big pollinating party. Odds are that, during mid-March, several warm and sunny days will allow insects to fly and plants to get the essential business of procreation behind them. Still it's a gamble, and a week of cold rain or several mornings of hard frost can mean few plums when July rolls around. The majority of March wildflowers spend far less energy on advertising and more on surviving the fickle season. Most are only a few inches tall and best appreciated through the use of a hand lens.

Tiny bluets flower profusely even though the weather remains highly uncertain, and my childhood favorite, the spring beauty, can form a pinkish white carpet only a few inches tall. A member of the portulaca family, spring beauties are star-shaped, white with pink tinting, and very pretty if you're willing to get down on the ground for a closer look. These little perennials sprout from a tuber that's half an inch to two inches in diameter and highly edible. A pinkish field of spring beauties can come to resemble a construction zone if a hungry bear decides to dine on this underground larder; according to some anthropologists, North American Indians gathered them as a welcome spring food source. Today the nutritional value of spring beauties is mostly forgotten, and Mother Nature's vernal flowers serve as a fueling station for small insects and a reminder to winter-weary children that warmth is only weeks away.

By March 16, there's already a hint of pink flowers gracing the redbud trees, and a Hominy Creek pool echoes with the keening of wood ducks. The drakes are regal in their russet reds, iridescent greens, warm fawn browns, and ivories, while the drab hens contemplate bankside trees, scanning each for convenient nesting cavities. The buffy hens do their nest searching while an eastern phoebe perches on a boxelder limb, occasionally darting out a few feet to snare one of the many midges active over the stream on this balmy afternoon.

For the moment all is tranquil, and it seems that March has morphed into May with the aid of a gentle nod from the weather gods. Yet

Ferns Prone to Take a Stroll

within twenty-four hours, all could change to ice or snow, the lingering final act of a weather system that began as a severe thunderstorm, maybe even a tornado. Survival during the days preceding the equinox hinges on the ability to hunker down and wait out schizoid weather. The systems swing through quickly and change can be abrupt, as March advances toward April in tentative steps, including some that may require backtracking.

In his book *Talking to the Moon*, Osage historian John Joseph Mathews explained that the Osages called the March moon the Just-Doing-That Moon, a lunar cycle so moody that they were at a loss for words when asked to explain in English. The cattle ranchers who followed the Osages into the tallgrass were just as perplexed by the weather as the Osages were. The new grass of April was money in the bank, and both groups watched the clouds with fingers crossed. Sooner or later the green fire of the growing season was bound to swell within prairie earth, and as the days grew longer little ground-hugging flowers amid the bleached winter grasses yielded to more robust species as Indiangrass, switchgrass, and the bluestems shot up inch by inch following April thunderstorms.

RENEWAL AT A SLOW BURN

Early in the spring, much of the Flint Hills grassland takes on a smoky haze and an acrid odor as ranchers set fire to the prairie. Burns are scheduled for days when the breeze is light and the humidity high, resulting in a blaze that burns low and slow and is more easily controlled.

People here have been burning grasslands since long before Columbus. Native Americans used fire to encourage the growth of new green grass, which in turn attracted the animals they utilized for food, shelter, and tools. Fire keeps woody growth in check and provides fertilizer by converting the previous growing season's leaves and stems to ashes.

Flint Hills ranchers, borrowing a page from their predecessors, burn old growth in the spring when the sun starts to climb higher in the sky, days are warming, and spring thunderstorms are either under way or soon to occur. By removing the dry plant material, ranch managers leave a swath of blackened bare earth that soaks up heat. Warming soils, nurtured by spring showers, erupt with the tender green shoots that cattle covet.

It's not unusual on a calm March afternoon to see cowboys on four-wheelers, dripping liquid fire on bleached brown grassland. Part of the process includes building firebreaks along fence lines, so that flames won't consume any wooden posts. Pickup trucks equipped with water tanks and sprayers await, insurance against the fire spreading beyond established perimeters. As the sun goes down, the orange-red fire line seems to burn into outer space as it crawls over dark hills and drops into even darker valleys. Now and then an eastern redcedar, an evergreen juniper common to the region, catches fire and erupts like Fourth of July fireworks. When a big pasture of two to three thousand acres goes under the torch, the spectacle is breathtaking and almost otherworldly.

At the same time, the smoke and the smell are a summons to winged predators. Hawks arrive like boys excited by rumors of a schoolyard fight. At times it seems that you can almost see the anticipation in the birds' eyes and sense the adrenaline pumping as they seek out a perch on a fence line, utility pole, or nearby oak, mostly something tall and as close to the fire as possible. From this vantage point, the hawks crane to see what the fire flushes into the open in front of the flames. Rats, mice, rabbits, and voles scramble for safety as the fire draws near, all terrified by the creeping conflagration. As a result, they fail to notice death descending from above—winged last rites in the form of one of nature's most highly proficient dive-bombers.

The following morning, these burned pastures will be at their bleakest, a blackened stretch of undulating earth pocked by thin columns of smoke rising from thousands of smoldering cow patties, those gray ovals of dried dung once used for fuel by pioneers. Scavengers, from crows to blackbirds to flocks of longspurs, walk the ashy aftermath searching for morsels ranging from blackened mouse to fried grasshopper. Yet this scorched Hades recovers quickly, especially if a rain shower helps push tiny new grass shoots toward sunlight. Within weeks, barring an unforeseen cold spell, the endless black will evolve into emerald, a shade so bright it seems electrified, a color that burns into the mind with its vibrant greenness.

According to a wildlife biologist friend, the timing of prescribed burning can alter the components of a grassland community. The rule of thumb, he said, was that spring burning favors the development of grasses (why ranchers burn in the spring) while autumn burning favors forbs (nonwoody, leafy, flowering plants). Wildlife managers are more apt to burn in autumn or sometimes in the middle of the summer to invigorate plant communities and encourage the growth of wildlife-friendly plants. Others condemn the practice due to the collateral damage to box turtles, reptiles, and ground-nesting birds.

On the other hand, the rebound in the numbers and species of ticks sometimes makes it easier to strike that match, especially now that tick-borne illnesses are proliferating. There were no ticks to speak of when I was a kid in the nineteen fifties, and we never used—nor had we ever heard of—insect repellent. Then the numbers of white-tailed deer began to rebound in our county. Ticks were definitely in the environment and hungry by the time I reached my twenties. A local rancher, blaming the explosion in the tick population on the explosion in the deer population, said he planned to resume annual burning in an effort to keep the arachnids in check.

Friends living in the dense hardwood forests of the Arkansas Ozarks point out that their grandparents burned the woods every year to control tick numbers. But in the Ozarks, where the forest shades mostly thin, rocky soil, organic enrichment depends on humus derived from decaying plant material, mostly the leaves that drift to the ground each autumn. According to the *American Heritage Science Dictionary*, humus is a dark brown or black organic substance made up of decayed plant or animal matter that provides nutrients for plants and increases the ability of soil to retain water. Obviously a healthy forest needs humus, and burning destroys the organic matter before it has an opportunity to make a necessary biological contribution.

So, to paraphrase the English poet Francis Thompson, it truly is difficult to metaphorically pluck a flower without troubling a star. To burn or not to burn, that may be the eternally nagging question. The practice doesn't happen without side effects, and some of them can be harmful, especially if you're managing a small relic prairie and trying to foster rare endemic species that can't recolonize from neighboring grassland.

Ranchers and biologists who manage grassland on a scale of thousands of acres understand from trial-and-error experience that prairie doesn't stay prairie very long or very well without the aid of fire and/or grazing. Thatch buildup from multiyear accumulations of dead grasses along with brush encroachment is a certainty without treatment, including a prescribed burn and a hungry cow or, as in the case of the Nature Conservancy's Tallgrass Prairie Preserve, the buffalo. There the staff burns both spring and autumn to keep new grass available for grazers. And by burning in patchy patterns in early spring, they leave dried grass islands of tall cover that the ground-nesting birds need to fledge offspring.

We don't have any textbooks left over from the Indians to tell us how, when, and where to burn to best benefit our grasslands. But we do have observations from early explorers who, upon entering the prairies, routinely marveled over the great numbers and variety of wildlife they saw and the amount of "firing the prairie" that took place and that seemed to be a common occurrence.

So it would seem that fire has long been an effective tool, at least in our grasslands and maybe in parts of our woodlands as well. Today the looming questions remain: where, when, and how much? There's concern that burning fence line to fence line every spring is good for cattle but detrimental to grassland birds. At the same time, our grasslands need the grazers they evolved with to maintain long-term health. So the work of biologists at places like the Tallgrass Prairie Preserve certainly seems essential to finding the happy medium that promotes good prairie health.

A SONG OF WIND AND CHANGING SEASONS

Spring burning season on the prairie coincides with the sound of upland sandpipers overhead, the males proclaiming the nesting territory they'll protect following a winter in South America. The migration journey, from as far away as the pampas of Argentina, covers thousands of miles, many of them over open water. Therefore these international aviators eagerly drop out of the sky, content to stride on long yellow legs across blackened grassland, seeking a tidbit that's generally very well done but tasty to a veteran traveler.

The birds return to the newly greening earth amid the earliest of the ground-hugging spring flowers. Sometimes it's a sunny day when a warm south wind pours over the prairie and ambient birdsong seems riotous. Yet just as often it's a day that's steely silent when winter lingers raw and bitter, the season strung out on low dark clouds and north winds that hint of snow rather than violets and buttercups.

Either way, these voyagers from the Southern Hemisphere descend upon the tallgrass on the wings of rapid change. It's as if upland sandpipers actually believe that these remaining native prairies, these limestone hills of Kansas and northern Oklahoma, are programmed to erupt into seasonal change immediately upon their arrival. If a bird's sheer biological presence could somehow manage the comings and goings of the seasons, then the flight of these intercontinental migrants with their boomerang wings would tug at the Earth in its orbit, transforming raw prairies into a perfect place for transients with nesting duties to perform.

Lengthening daylight demands urgency from grassland-loving shorebirds that leave South American wintering grounds in February, arrive on the Texas Gulf Coast by March, and then spread out across America's grassland interior, intent upon the serious business of establishing nesting territory by late March or early April. Their arrival coincides with the first rapidly greening grasses and early flowering forbs. Upland sandpipers exhibit a sense of purpose that devours miles and endures storms. Theirs is the total commitment of a marathon flier that may weigh up to seven ounces, stand twelve inches tall, and journey across continents on wings that stretch tip to tip to around twenty inches. A drab mix of buff, brown, and gray, the upland sandpiper shares the muted plumage of most of its shorebird clan. Yet it's a marvel of flight with a voice to match, most notably when broadcasting sandpiper song above spring meadows in a stirring liquid vibrato, insisting that it's time for the world to reawaken now that an undeniable sandpiper presence has arrived to set up housekeeping.

Some of the sandpipers return to the prairie already paired, many to the same annual nesting area in this wide, rolling expanse of shallow rock and native grasses. Oftentimes the new arrivals prefer to oversee their surroundings from atop a handy fence post. Such perches of weathered wood or rusty steel generally offer the most prominent vertical objects in a typically horizontal landscape. The birds settle on top of each perch on spindly legs and, upon landing, keep both wings vertical for just a moment, as if uncertain what to do with them.

Next the birds fold each wing carefully. It seems a conscious effort, like a fussy mother rearranging clothes after they've been tossed aside by a self-absorbed teenager. Yet the wing-folding ritual pales before the territorial flight and the sweet, sad music that accompanies each fluttering circle among earth, clouds, and sun.

The flight to their prairie nesting grounds is direct and strong, and the birds are equipped with an admirable wingspan designed to accomplish such a task. Upon arrival, time spent airborne revolves around the perimeter of each sandpiper's chosen territory. The birds practically hover at times on stiff, rapidly vibrating wings, more like hummingbirds than transoceanic travelers. And while its flight may spiral upward so high that the sandpiper gets lost against the clouds, its haunting call never seems to fade from hearing.

Upland sandpiper song begins with a bubbly, rising tremolo that suddenly breaks into a long, shrill wolf whistle, the key minor, the pitch high. It's a sound that can cause kids fishing along the banks of farm ponds to stare skyward, even as their bobbers dance a catfish jig. The cry of the upland sandpiper has amazing carrying power to match the vastness of the prairie's undulating hills. It's a song perfected with a big landscape in mind, each note in harmony with the booming of prairie-chickens dancing below and the sad murmuring of mourning doves cooing their poignant territorial music.

Mated upland sandpiper pairs generally choose a clump of the previous year's dry prairie grass as nesting cover, sometimes pulling the stems low to help conceal the slight scrape, which contains an average of four eggs. The male is attentive to the female, and chicks hatch some twenty-four days after the final egg is laid. During a fledging period of around a month, the long-legged chicks ramble the grasslands along with their parents, learning the diet and prairie ways of the upland sandpiper tribe. Early summer in the tallgrass can present a smorgasbord of grasshoppers, crickets, and other insect fare. Young birds scramble through grasses and beneath flowers like miniature ostriches. Yet the chicks are quicker to escape than one might suppose, able to effectively vanish from sight by remaining motionless, essentially becoming a sandpiper version of a rock or a dollop of dry cow or buffalo dung.

According to Arthur Cleveland Bent and the data he assembled in *Life Histories of North American Shore Birds*, upland sandpipers were hunted nearly into oblivion during the late nineteenth century and almost suffered a fate similar to that of Eskimo curlews and passenger pigeons. Bent recounts old newspaper stories relating how in Manson, Iowa, in 1889, "prairie plovers" sold for 10 cents per bird. During the 1880s prices in Spirit Lake, Iowa, hovered around $1.25 per dozen, and the bird was rarely seen in the state after 1910. A lucrative market resulted in fifty to sixty thousand upland sandpipers being shipped annually from Nebraska in the years from about 1870 to around 1890, the birds bound for stores and restaurants in eastern cities. As late as 1912, sandpipers were shipped by the barrel in rail cars to Chicago markets, where those who could afford the price dined on "plover on toast."

While Eskimo curlews and passenger pigeons never recovered from late nineteenth-century market hunting, the upland sandpiper managed to slowly renew its numbers, clinging tenaciously to life in America's remaining native grasslands. The fact that the bird escaped the fate of other marketable birds seems even more amazing when you consider that "plover" was also a culinary treat on the South American pampas where the sandpipers winter.

But somehow the shorebird turned prairie dweller managed to survive. Upland sandpipers, along with long-billed curlews and mountain plovers, comprise a trio of shorebirds that evolved an inland breeding strategy that lifted them beyond shorelines and into interior grasslands, with the prairies providing ample space and a rich supply of insect protein. All three survived the era of market hunting only to once again suffer a decline in numbers when native grasslands were plowed under.

Autumn staging and migration begin soon after upland sandpiper chicks are fledged, but it is a leisurely journey compared to the directness of the spring flight. Southbound birds flock to food sources, building energy reserves for the long journey back to the pampas. And then, when the time and the weather are right, they launch into the immensity of the sky above, following moon or stars, magnetic fields, or some biological memory that leads them across oceans, bound for the balmy days that await south of the equator.

I've heard these birds' autumn flight calls from South Dakota to southeastern Colorado to deep into Texas, a poignant whistle that fits perfectly with weather moods ranging from a light frost to a thunderstorm. The sound has, like that of geese passing overhead, a sense of longing inherent in each syllable. Sometimes it's hard to see the skybound traveler, but still each melancholy call comes through clearly, announcing that another green season has run its course. It's a serene cry, fit for a small bird on a big journey, a testament to all those landlocked below that, for a moment at least, all is well in the world of upland sandpipers.

After that, there's little to do but wait. It will be months before the drab bird with the mystical voice once again hovers overhead like a miniature helicopter, regaling the world with majestic flute tunes. But when upland sandpipers return from the Argentine, it's hark the herald angels sing for those of us who haven't heard such music for more than half a year. And when the new arrival settles onto a fence post and painstakingly stores each wing like a maestro encasing a Stradivarius, the scene becomes classic living sculpture, true tallgrass prairie art evolved out of gray limestone and rapidly greening grass.

It's still a week until the equinox, the day when thoughts of spring become official if not totally dependable, and when length of daylight and darkness becomes equal. However, this breezy day along the headwaters of Hominy Creek feels very much as if winter has been banished, as south winds coax mid-afternoon temperatures into the sixties. A flock of Harris's sparrows, eight birds altogether with four showing the black bibs of mature males, is foraging in several elms near steep limestone bluffs bordering the stream. At this time of the year, the oval seeds on the trees are dull green and easily mistaken for the early leaves that won't actually appear until April. The density of the seeds gives the valley a green tint that corresponds to the increased bird activity.

Harris's sparrows are large members of their tribe, somber in black and brown feathers and sounding a bit melancholy due to the minor key whistles that provide an audible link to the group's social order. The birds winter in the south-central United States and nest on the tundra in northern Canada. Their bills are pinkish, and their black crowns and bibs contrast with the chestnut brown backs and white breasts. Wingspans may reach to 10.6 inches, with an overall body length of as much as 7.9 inches.

Harris's sparrows hang around into May here on the southern prairies, giving the frozen north a chance to thaw before they begin their spring migration. Due to the remoteness of the birds' breeding ground, no one knew exactly where they reared their young until ornithologist and bird artist George Miksch Sutton found a nest near Churchill, Manitoba, in 1931.

The oldest males in each flock are generally dominant and also show the greatest amount of black in their bibs. Dominant males are afforded the best opportunities for foraging and roosting sites. The mellow whistles, earthy beauty, and apparent gentleness of these sparrows have earned them many fans among birders, including people who travel great distances to add this long-distance traveler to their life list.

The warming afternoon has summoned another birdlike voice from the pools bordering the main channels of the stream. Strecker's chorus frogs, stubby, toadlike little creatures that can grow up to an inch and a half long, tend to be early breeders and may begin to call following thunderstorms as early as February. From a distance the summons seems high and shrill and almost supernaturally loud, considering the size of the callers. But when you draw closer, the high-pitched pleading contains a noticeable hoarseness plus a back-and-forth, pulleylike separation of phrases. Chorus frogs must attract mates, breed, and have their eggs hatch and their tadpoles mature before spring pools dry up during summer. Therefore, the alacrity in their calls represents notes forged in biological earnestness and evolution.

Eastern bluebirds are also early nesters, and this afternoon at least six males are vocally marking their territory amid a post oak grove not far from the stream. The grove contains several standing dead trunks with holes excavated by woodpeckers. Some of the fire-killed trunks contain as many as four excellent nesting cavities.

The gentle bluebird of folklore and human fancy is as different from the creature dwelling in these hollowed-out oaks as a *Tyrannosaurus rex* is from a teddy bear. In reality these handsome little prairie dwellers mainly represent survival of the fittest, and they jockey and battle for nesting territory like blue-clad gladiators. Eye-appealing they may well be, but they're all bird below those lovely feathers and borderline reptilian in their quest to eat, mate, rear young, and stay alive while they do it.

I once watched a male bluebird go after a small lizard, a juvenile five-lined skink that wandered into the open at an inopportune time. The bird spotted the dark reptile with its bright blue tail, an appealing appendage designed as a predator target, a fleshy extension engineered to break away under duress while allowing the young skink to flee unscathed. But this bluebird was much too experienced for that ruse. He grabbed the skink mid-body, battered it against a rock, then tore it in half, offering a portion to his mate. *T. rex* itself couldn't have achieved such savage butchery in such a short time. Yet it was all in a lunchtime's work for a small bird facing the daunting task of passing along genes to progeny, totally unaware of all the peace, love, and happiness bestowed upon its anthropomorphic image.

During a territorial battle fought on the wing in the oak grove, one of the male bluebirds and his rival vanish into a shadow cast by a big mound of clouds, one of many sailing overhead during this week of seasonal weather shifting. These drifting cumulous sky islands, each a giant dollop of white tinged with gray, have a summertime look to them, a scalloped whipped cream demeanor. In a few months such clouds might prelude a dramatic weather event should they darken, mushroom into towering thunderheads, and become the precursors of a tornado.

But today they are just clouds, drifting along like boats on a lake, creating shadows that slide over the dormant brown of a countryside weary of winter. Life beneath the clouds verges on restlessness as the afternoon temperature climbs higher into the sixties.

Downy serviceberry trees are flowering a cottony white along the boulder-strewn rim of Hominy Creek, a cheery sight against the drab browns and grays of late winter. This member of the rose family, also known as shadbush, shadblow, Juneberry, sarvis, and other colloquialisms, carries the scientific moniker *Amelanchier arborea*. The five-petaled white flowers that brighten the tree before the leaves emerge produce a dark blue fruit, a berry that wild creatures relish. I've rarely managed to beat the birds to these sweet berries when they ripen, but on the other hand it's heartening to know that nutritious bounty is available during the height of the season when so many creatures are exhausting themselves in an effort to rear young.

One serviceberry tree, a particularly large specimen, casts a shadow over the spot where a little spring-fed creek tumbles over a rocky ledge, dropping fifteen feet or so into a shaded canyon. After a quarter mile of bouncing over rocks and ledges, the little stream enters Hominy Creek and begins a journey to the Verdigris River, then the Arkansas, then the Mississippi, then the Atlantic Ocean. Here, amid the silence of tall-grass prairie, water rising from the earth near a little oak grove where white-tailed deer like to bed down quickly rushes away on a journey that will carry it thousands of miles. It's a solemn thought, one to be mulled over while standing at the brink of a beautiful waterfall as the allure of serviceberry flowers teases winged pollinators of varied sizes and descriptions. Such a journey would be a marvelous adventure to undertake, but it's hard to imagine that any place along the way could be more restful than this one.

Water in the catchment pool at the bottom of the waterfall is writhing with both turbulence and the biological manifestation of seasonal change. Crayfish, most of them five or six inches in length, are mingling in the pool. The little crustaceans, each bright red-orange, have few obligations other than to live out the simple destiny of their species. Generally, that includes being eaten.

Crayfish of this size are like the meatballs within the spaghetti for fish dwelling in the Hominy Creek pools. Green sunfish, channel catfish, largemouth bass, all are as addicted to this down-home form of lobster tail as any Cajun is said to be. Knowledgeable anglers long ago figured out that "crawdads" are the bait to turn to for bragging-size bass, while those who reject live bait as unsporting stock up on both hard and soft plastic crayfish imitations.

Other crayfish connoisseurs include raccoon, mink, herons, egrets, and water snakes, essentially any creature that desires food that combines high protein, excellent flavor, and ubiquitous presence. These adaptable, almost buglike stream dwellers comprise a large part of the freshwater commissary in pools such as this one. Bass will feast until crayfish pinchers are dangling from their mouths. I've been told that, in Louisiana, aficionados of crayfish jambalaya tend to do the same.

On an evening in mid-April, the moisture-laden air lay heavy upon the land. Winds grew calm, and weather forecasters urged viewers to be prepared for what could become tornadic outbreaks. Strong thunderstorms were poised to sweep over the southern Flint Hills, with particularly heavy storms occurring along a line paralleling the Kansas-Oklahoma border. Prior to the severe weather warning, afternoon temperatures had climbed into the eighties, while a strong south wind pulled moisture north from the Gulf of Mexico. The impending storms would develop along a frontal boundary pushing down from the north. Cold air clashed with a mountain of atmospheric warmth and humidity, and the skies erupted.

In the hours prior to the storms, moody calls of mourning doves swirled on a breeze rising above new green shoots of Indiangrass, switchgrass, and bluestems. Killdeer scurried through the early spring growth, the adult birds nagging at chicks that seemed little more than cotton balls perched on piano wire legs. One of the chicks, scampering on spindly appendages, caught its bill on a grass stem, somersaulted, bounced back up, and raced away unhurt, showing the resiliency of youth and provoking a fretting, keening cry from the mother bird.

Late that evening, a glowering eyebrow of sunlight painted a low line of clouds fiery orange. Ominous, towering clouds were building, and shortly after midnight lightning lit up the sky just as a burst of wind made nearby cottonwood trees tremble. Three inches of rain fell before daybreak, with intermittent storms continuing in the form of brief heavy showers. By late afternoon ditches and fields stood in water, and the first major frog and toad chorus of spring rent the air.

The epicenter of this amphibian orgy was an old field not far from the Arkansas River. It had been farmed for a few years, then allowed to stand idle for decades. Some of the native grasses had returned, along with the annual forbs that prosper following disruption. Old cropland terraces, grown up in grass, now served as levees for the mini-lakes that filled the depressions.

Through bursts of amphibian squalling announcing another pending cloudburst, I watched as Great Plains toads moved across county roads like ancient mariners summoned to a siren's song. Eventually the sun sank into a night that promised to remain warm, wet, and windy, perfect for an anuran bacchanal.

Male toads settled into the shallow pools trapped in the abandoned farm field, where they regaled the darkness with long high-pitched trills. Joining the chorus were much smaller Great Plains narrow-mouthed toads and some tiny spotted chorus frogs, the latter adding their sheeplike bleats and brassy, hiccuping quacks to the overall repertoire.

A great horned owl hooted from riverside cottonwoods during the lulls among lightning flashes, thunder, and brief downpours. A chuck-will's-widow repeated its namesake call while dark and moody skies rumbled with thunder. It was a wild night, devoid of mercury vapor lights and automobile sounds, the only human disturbance the occasional beam from my flashlight.

A century and a half ago, similarly swirling wind and rain most likely did little to drown out the grunts of thousands of buffalo made nervous by a storm. Countless buffalo wallows would have glistened beneath each lightning strike, the shallow depressions filled to overflowing like saucers under a faucet, each ready to serve as a predator-free frog and toad nursery. Today's breeding pools are likely to result from human impact on the land rather than wallowing buffalo, but standing water is standing water whether it's in the form of a buffalo wallow or a borrow ditch. A shallow rain-drenched pool still tugs like a magnet at these subterranean-dwelling prairie choristers, urging toads and tiny frogs by the thousands to answer an undeniable biological call.

Sometimes here in the tallgrass country, these perfect storms may skip a year or more before the precise combination of temperature and rainfall is sufficient to fill the temporary breeding pools and summon the singers. A warm night is best, generally in April or May well past the average annual date of the final freeze. It will be a night when thunderstorms drench the grasslands with the potential for more to come, leaving ample water in the pools until the tadpoles metamorphose.

Permanent standing water is avoided because permanent water has permanent residents with appetites, some eager to dine on a surfeit of frog and toad spawn. Therefore, reproductive odds are best when the amphibians lay their eggs in temporary pools. In the late nineteenth century, after the buffalo disappeared, our prairies lost much of the wild banshee wailing that once reverberated during spring storms from Mexico north to the Canadian prairie provinces.

Before the arrival of cow and plow, the trills, bleats, and vibrato clicks of all these amphibians in love would have been accented by the whinny of lesser yellowlegs on the wing, the sad whistles of curlews, and the soft quacks of migrating teal. Prior to settlement, the prairie was a place that liked its music loud and lots of instruments in its orchestra. The compositions were classic opera with an emphasis on birth, death, and the continuity of species. This was a song that can still be heard, albeit less rowdily, in relic pools in relic meadows, where ancient amphibian races still gather to defy what appears to be an uncertain future.

Loudest and most numerous of the serenaders on this particular stormy night were the Great Plains toads, native to grasslands from the Flint and Osage Hills west to the arid Southwest. Secretive burrowers except at breeding time, Great Plains toads emerge at night to feed on insects. Yet on this particular lightning-lashed evening, thoughts of food were distant as the males produced a pleading, almost deafening concert. The toads, averaging two to four inches in length, were unnervingly loud, their hoarse trills almost drowning out the tornado-warning sirens sounding in the distance. The hormone-infused amphibians wailed at a high pitch, each tremolo blast lasting up to fifty seconds per trill.

The males, well camouflaged with green spots scattered over a background of yellow, cream, or gold, launched their serenades with a single hiccuping note that quickly burst into the main high-volume call. At the end of each aria, the singer trailed off into silence with a few short jerky trills, as if ratcheting down to breathlessness. It was a wild bansheelike performance, perfectly in sync with the strong south winds, lightning strikes, and the sound of thunder in the distance. The trilling continued through the night, at a volume that seemed loud enough to summon toad kinfolk all the way from West Texas. At times, the flooded outdoor amphitheater swelled with an entire orchestra of frog and toad symphony once the spotted chorus frogs and Great Plains narrow-mouthed toads added their particular voices.

The narrow-mouthed toads were much smaller and quieter than their Great Plains relatives yet nonetheless distinctive with their vocals. They launched each solo with a sharp, chick-like peep, followed by a buzzing bleat that sounded like a cross between an insect and a sheep. The sound carried well for an animal barely an inch long, a stubby, alien-looking little creature with a fold of olive-colored skin that circled the back of its blunt head and snout. By midnight, dozens of these small toads were calling from the dark green sedge tussocks rising a few inches above the narrow pools. Narrow-mouthed toads increase breeding success by laying eggs that hatch quickly, resulting in tadpoles that metamorphose within two months.

The smallest carolers in this midnight chorale were perhaps the most beautiful. Spotted chorus frogs, only three-quarters of an inch to an inch and a quarter long, clung to the security of sedge clumps as they delivered their raspy, staccato calls. Each tiny grassland deni- zen displayed a dorsal pattern of bright green spots over larger golden tan disks that lit up like jewels in my flashlight beam. Their call was a rapidly repeated, low-pitched, husky "wank" that added a thumping rhythm section to the combination of bleats and trills, filling the wet meadow with a bewitching anuran ensemble.

When the mating rains were over, all three species of amphibians would return to the cool recesses of their daytime burrows, either bor- rowing shelter from other animals or digging their own. The Great Plains toad is an accomplished digger, while the diminutive nar- row-mouthed toad prefers to share space with others under rocks or in rodent burrows, sometimes in the company of spiders as large as tarantulas, and the chorus frog probably retreats to available burrows.

Narrow-mouthed toads are ant-eating specialists, the other two general insectivores. But on this spring evening, all they cared about was summoning a female they could clasp tightly with their forelegs, adding sperm to each clump of eggs laid in the pools. Even the tiny spotted chorus frogs might fertilize as many as a thousand eggs, laid in small jellylike masses of around thirty eggs each, all attached to plant stems just below the water's surface. Their eggs would hatch in two to ten days depending upon weather conditions, the process a race against time and the desiccating powers of wind and sunlight. If all went well, the tadpoles would mature into tiny spotted chorus frogs before their pool evaporated. If not, then in time another storm would follow and the grassland-dwelling amphibians would try again.

Great Plains toads take advantage of their reproductive opportunities by being as fecund as they are loud and insistent. Each female lays a mass of eggs that may number as many as 45,000, her output contingent upon her body size. These prairie toads are quick to respond to thunderstorms that present breeding potential, remaining ready to mate from around the first of April to the end of September.

Time from freshly fertilized egg to emerging Great Plains toadlet can be as short as some three weeks or as long as seven weeks. It all depends upon sunlight, rain, and the rich organic soup that nurtures the egg to tadpole to toadlet cycle. Pollution takes a toll on toad and frog reproduction, as does death by natural causes—including predators like giant water bugs. An almond-shaped inch and a half of aquatic appetite, this bug likes nothing better than to snag a tadpole, insert a mouthpart, inject an enzyme that breaks down tissue, and then sip the results.

Frogs and toads counter by overwhelming the breeding pools with great numbers of offspring. Judging from both velocity and din, this stormy night would be conducive to an epic breeding event. Around midnight the thunder grew louder, the amphibians cranked up the volume, and the lightning revealed another squall line surging south. Within minutes the rain was pouring from celestial buckets, and the reinvigorated congregation of springtime carolers reached an almost painful volume. What they were saying wasn't exactly a page from a prairie hymnal but more like something I'd imagine from the glory days of Stonehenge. Basically it was the sound of ancient existence being renewed, a pristine performance in an ageless setting. Few things on this planet can showcase a lust for life more powerfully than that.

Early spring in the Flint and Osage Hills is a time of restless energy. Migrants whinny overhead. Frogs and toads bleat, chirp, and rattle. Wild turkey strut, greater prairie-chickens dance, and eastern collared lizards beguile the eye like abstract art in their blue and yellow breeding colors.

As the hills renew spring growth, cattle arrive from the grass-deprived plains of West Texas. Cowboys on horseback sort steers and drive them by the hundreds to awaiting greener pastures. And on warm and balmy afternoons, snakes crawl out from underneath slabs of rock, bask in the sun, and watch the proceedings with unblinking eyes. So much is happening all at once that it's a tsunami of renewal, a sensory overload accented by ungulate appetites.

For my father, it was a time to be fishing. He'd walk the banks of ponds, noting the direction of the wind, the temperature, the water clarity, what birds were moving, and then he'd catch fish—lots of them. He loved fishing, but I think angling was also an excuse for simply being outdoors and watching wildlife. Back home he'd share tales of the animals and birds he'd seen, and little went undetected. He'd spent a lifetime in this tallgrass prairie country and grown to be a part of it, a man serenely at home in his surroundings.

Early one morning following a fishing trip, he returned at a loss to explain some birds he'd seen searching for food in an April pasture. I was home from college, and we drove back out to the brown and green plaid prairie, hoping to obtain a closer look.

More than forty-five years have passed since that day when several shorebirds launched skyward and rowed into the wind on fluttering wings. They were smaller than long-billed curlews yet showed the modestly curved bill and simple brown plumage of the curlew tribe. I didn't know much about shorebirds at the time, and I certainly didn't know anything about Eskimo curlews. However, the birds we watched as they circled overhead resembled a painting in a book I borrowed from the library, enough so that I dared to dream the impossible, and I continue to do so until this day.

According to the U.S. Fish and Wildlife Service the Eskimo curlew, *Numenius borealis*, is or was a medium-size wading bird averaging around twelve inches long, with a slender, slightly curved bill. A dark crown, pale crown stripe, cinnamon highlights, brown barring, and bluish gray legs comprise the commonly accepted description given for this former prairie migrant. Unfortunately, most of what we know about the Eskimo curlew comes from museum specimens. Not many live birds have been seen, much less identified, in our lifetimes. Eskimo curlews were subjected to indiscriminate slaughter more than a hundred years ago, and today the birds most likely are extinct.

That sad fact didn't diminish my curiosity as research revealed the scope of the tragedy. According to Arthur Cleveland Bent in his *Life Histories of North American Shore Birds*, one observer reported Flint Hills prairies "fairly alive" with Eskimo curlews between March 25 and April 2, 1884. I read anecdotes about curlews in flocks numbering in the thousands migrating north and how hunters oftentimes wasted many of the birds they killed, figuring that the numbers were so great there could be no end to them.

But the birds were exterminated just the same, suffering the same fate as the passenger pigeon, the Carolina parakeet, and other species once considered too numerous to destroy, yet in the end unable to cope with the wholesale market hunting and habitat alteration of the late 1800s.

The great flocks of Eskimo curlews were birds of the past by the turn of the twentieth century. After that only a few were seen, and those sightings were sporadic in nature. I found a 1948 sighting for

Oklahoma, but I can't confirm the validity. It was in mid-April, some seventeen miles west of Pawhuska, around the same place where I saw the small curlew-like birds I couldn't identify in the early 1970s.

Modern reports of Eskimo curlews have been rare, especially sightings by people with the birding experience that allows their sightings to be taken seriously. More often than not, modern Eskimo curlew reports turn out to be their larger cousin, the whimbrel. However, for years even a single wishful observation was tantalizing enough to cause some birders to prolong the inevitable conclusion. The less romantic believe that Eskimo curlews are extinct or, even if a few remain, past the point of recovery.

Few who find solace in wild creatures and wild places want to believe that humankind is capable of mostly destroying, in about twenty years' time, a species that migrated through the nation's midland prairies by the millions. Witnesses to the late nineteenth-century migrations said Eskimo curlew flocks formed dense masses extending a quarter to half a mile long and a hundred yards wide. Bent reported that when birds in these flocks cupped their wings and landed on the prairie, they'd darken forty to fifty acres.

After settlers and shotguns arrived on the grasslands, the curlews touched down at their peril. "The gentle birds ran the gauntlet all of their migration, and no one lifted a finger to protect them until it was too late," recalled Bent. "They were so gentle, so confiding, so full of sympathy for their fallen companions that, in closely packed ranks, they fell easy victims to the carnage."

Eskimo curlews migrated from southern South America to nest on the northern Arctic coast. From the Arctic, the birds flew east as far as Labrador before launching their transoceanic flight back south of the equator. It was a journey requiring strong flight over thousands of miles and the consumption of a massive amount of calories. During spring migration, the curlews were fond of grasshoppers and grasshopper eggs, probing in the soil for the latter with curved bills fifty to sixty millimeters in length.

When pioneers arrived with mules and plows, the birds dropped onto freshly turned fields to feast on grubs and worms. It's possible that Eskimo curlews dined on agricultural pests to such an extent that they provided an invaluable service to farmers. Unfortunately, the birds provided something even more beneficial—easily harvested protein and quite tasty protein at that. Eskimo curlews were said to be delicious, often so fat during autumn migration that the breasts of birds killed on the wing burst open upon hitting the ground. They sold by the barrel in the growing cities of the East, providing a delicacy that earned market hunters a little hard currency in a cash-strapped world.

Eskimo curlews were easily enough killed. Bent tells of hunters on the Kansas and Nebraska prairies shooting into huge flocks and dropping so many birds that they filled wagons equipped with sideboards. When more curlews descended and the shooting resumed, the wagons were dumped and refilled, leaving piles of dead curlews to rot on the ground.

"If disturbed they will frequently alight again at no great distance, if not previously harassed, and . . . they can be approached at all times, for they are either very tame or very shy," one hunter explained. Another told of firing an old muzzle-loading shotgun into a flock of curlews. "A single shot brought down twenty-eight birds at once, and for the next half mile fatally wounded birds continued to drop to the ground." Most agreed that the compact flocks and tameness of the birds made such slaughter possible.

The advent of repeating firearms allowed the massacre to become even more pronounced, and the migrants shared traits that left them vulnerable to such carnage. They desperately needed to store calories for their extensive migration flights and remained extremely devoted to favorite feeding grounds. They also were loath to leave fellow birds killed or wounded by hunters, often circling over or landing next to fallen curlews and losing their own lives as a result.

Had they managed to hang on until 1916, Eskimo curlews would have received protection under the Migratory Bird Treaty Act. As it was, they were harassed and hunted eleven months of the year, killed for the market during their spring and autumn migrations and on their wintering grounds in South America. And as Cornell University's Lab of Ornithology points out, the curlews became favorite targets of market hunters when the passenger pigeon, another native bird that once darkened America's skies by the millions, was shot into extinction.

Before Europeans arrived on this continent, an April sunrise on the prairie would have unveiled an American wildlife utopia. The distances would have been occupied by buffalo and elk, with buffalo wolves trailing the herds, coyotes rummaging for leftovers, prairie grouse displaying, bears digging roots, hawks circling, eagles soaring, sandhill and whooping cranes resting during migration. And scattered over the great grasslands, small curlews around twelve inches long would be descending in huge flocks, their soft, whistling calls mingling with the grunts, chirps, honks, and chatter of a landscape lavish with wildlife.

Now many of these species have been driven either into mountain sanctuaries or into extinction by our greed and our inability to see beyond the next year, the next month, even the next day. The Eskimo curlew, once the most numerous shorebird on the North American continent, was destroyed so that customers in restaurants could enjoy a delicacy. Compounding this travesty was an almost universal lack of remorse.

Still, some of us continue to carry the Eskimo curlew in our thoughts and in our hearts, especially in early spring when little ground-hugging flowers begin to bloom. Maybe a ghost of a chance remains that a small brown prayer of a bird will drop from the clouds and walk among the anemones, searching for grubs and grasshoppers and a new chance at life.

And at that moment, should such magic ever happen, another spring will seem far more splendid. The odds remain slim to none, of course. But then what is springtime without hope, given ample time to daydream amid rapidly greening pastures?

It's one of those afternoons that offer promise. Promise that the days actually are growing longer, that the last bitter winter blow may be history, that birds may soon sing again, that brown will yield to green, that native flowers will color the pale duff underfoot with verbena and phlox purple and mustard yellow and anemones the color of a radiant summer sky. It's all longing, of course. Great expectations born of the fact that it's still late winter, yet the thermometer has climbed to sixty on a practically balmy day.

Native plants are genetically programmed to be more cautious than my imagination on a day that feels like spring. The groundhog says six more weeks, and while I'm not inclined to trust a weather-forecasting rodent, I've learned from living on the prairie throughout what has been a reasonably long life that winter will nip at the heels of the growing season well into April. The only flowers prone to cast a rainbow shadow weeks before the vernal equinox are those brought here from somewhere else, flowers carefully planted by loving yet long-forgotten hands.

Daffodils are awakening today in remote locations along these late winter hillsides, despite the cold winds that prevailed until early this morning and a wan sun that's struggled to raise the temperature above freezing the past few days. It's still weeks away from official spring, yet some of the signs are in place—a temporary pool incubating the opaque globs of salamander eggs, an eastern phoebe in a willow by the pond awaiting afternoon midge swarms, skunks on the march, oblivious to busy highways.

A terse weather bulletin underscores the vicissitudes of the season: a high of 67 degrees one day falling to just above freezing the next. Even so, the daffodils unfurl with panache, consummating the business of being a flower during the warm days, surviving the cold snaps with customary daffodil hardiness.

Daffodils are not native here, yet they seem so common that most of us assume they've always been around to flower when the sun attempts its annual effort to wrest control from late winter. Even modern country homes seem almost naked without these waxy tubular flowers, most of them a rich butter yellow.

Jonquil is how they're known by most rural folk, a perfect flower to ward off winter blues, a colorful border plant to presage the heirloom roses yet to bloom. Bright yellow jonquils also are a gravesite choice, flowering before the end of the frosts, in place to brighten up a spring visit before relatives arrive in May toting armloads of artificial blossoms picked from the shelves of superstores.

These prairie hills have been as tough to live in as they are handsome to look upon, and stark evidence of those who labored and lost still remains—piles of rocks from nearby fields, stumps ensnarled in vines and shrubby second growth, a hole in the ground that once served as a cellar. And always there are daffodils. They're like Johnny Appleseed's trees, except they signify expectation eroding into resignation, a final resting place of futile hopes and dreams, fenced by golden flowers.

Narcissus is the name botanists prefer for these flowers on loan from Europe. Various texts cite anywhere from fifty to a hundred cultivated species, but it is the solid yellow variety that appears most commonly around abandoned homesteads. Immigrants brought daffodils with them from the Old World, and the plant marks their passage from east to west along a mountainous spine—the Appalachians, Alleghenies, and Ozarks—and out onto the prairies. Few newcomers could have chosen a more rugged path or a better keepsake to accompany them.

According to Greek mythology, Narcissus was a youth noted for his uncommon beauty. As legend has it, this young man knelt beside a pool and grew so enamored with his own reflection that he fell in and drowned. Afterward, the narcissus flower grew from the place where he died. The legend provided not only a name for the flower but also the root for the word "narcissism."

Yet "narcissistic" isn't a term that would apply to the settlers who struggled to survive on corn, potatoes, and beans until the bounty of the land eroded and entire families were forced to move on. Today small clearings remain where only daffodils grow, a testimonial to those who arrived with little more than an ax, a mule, a few seeds, and the clothes on their backs, content to mark time with a few flower bulbs carried west to remind them that winter wouldn't last forever.

Daffodils still flower near stone foundations built by hardscrabble farmers who gave in to the drought, the bank, and the indignity of it all during the Depression and then followed rumors west to California. The bright yellows of the flowers, pressed against the grays and bleached browns of late winter, provide an unspoken benediction for this forgotten trail of tears.

More and more I believe that daffodils are the corsage we pin on the lapel of our hard-handed ways with the landscape—the forested slopes carelessly shorn of timber, the streams strangled by silt, the cut and run, the plow and pray, hookworms and rickets, God's will be done in forgotten graveyards pocked with upright sandstone slabs scratched with dates indicating a lost loved one. And there to memorialize each nameless notation in some unwritten history remain a few daffodils, emerging from bulbs planted next to a doorway left behind, the last will and testament of generations stretching back over a thousand miles of downtrodden earth.

Sometimes scraps of a few old homesteads still stand to remind us of America's pioneer heritage, but oftentimes only daffodils remain in place to usher winter into spring and mark the poignancy of this ancestral passage. For a week or so when mostly bleakness reigns, the brown hills show streaks of gold, a reminder that someone passed this way before, daydreaming of an eternity of yellow flowers.

In his book *Konza Prairie: A Tallgrass Natural History*, O. J. Reichman explores the intricate underground associations that underscore the complexity of a grassland ecosystem. South of Manhattan, Kansas, Konza Prairie is a former Flint Hills cattle ranch purchased by the Nature Conservancy and used as a research station by Kansas State University. The preserve is a beautiful remnant of the original Flint Hills ecotype, where ongoing research has studied the interactions of grassland and fire, grazing by both cattle and buffalo, and prairie soil dynamics.

The soils of both the northern and southern Flint Hills are essentially the eroded residue of the region's limestone, sandstone, and shale geology, resulting from seawater inundations occurring periodically over hundreds of millions of years. Layers of bedrock tend to be thick while the soils are thin yet fertile, bad news for farmers and their plows but a benediction for those who love windswept grasslands and hope to protect what's left. Native prairie plants use their extensive root systems to colonize the stubborn skin of hills that, following a burn, may expose what appears to be a cracked tile of limestone or sandstone surface. Still, the grasses and forbs that prosper here are expert at mining the depths needed to survive during times of environmental stress.

They manage with roots that, if laid end to end, would stretch out for miles, each root aided by millions of tiny root hairs.

According to Reichman, these extremely fine root hairs are extensive. His book reveals that the roots of a single rye plant contained 14 million root hairs providing more than 4,000 square feet of surface area, or more square footage than two large family homes. These hairs have evolved a working relationship with stringy soil fungi called mycorrhizae, strands that help the plant absorb nutrients in exchange for a gift of carbohydrates from the parent plant. Giving back a little of what the mycorrhizae have provided is an excellent trade-off for the plant. Reichman's readers will discover that the inclusion of mycorrhizae in each plant's metabolic activities helps extend the zone of nutrient-seeking activity by at least a factor of five.

Research like that ongoing at Konza explores the notion that prairie plants can hook up with the fungi when in need or shut down this association entirely during times of stress, such as extended drought. When environmental conditions stabilize, the mycorrhizae once again aid prairie plants in securing vital minerals, including phosphorus. According to Reichman, Konza Prairie research with big bluestem revealed that introduced seedlings must either be fed phosphorus fertilizer to stay alive or inoculated with mycorrhizae so that the young bluestem specimens can obtain the life-giving mineral on their own. These symbiotic assistants have been discovered at work in association with prairie grass roots down to depths of seven feet, an indication of how extensive the mycorrhizae relationship actually is and how deeply prairie plants probe for the nutrients they need.

Nitrogen is a major element in plant health. Yet it can't be derived from the weathering of rocks and therefore isn't readily available in the soil. Instead, research has shown that prairie plants rely on atmospheric nitrogen, which doesn't exist in a form that plants can accommodate. To make this nitrogen both usable and available in the soil, plants have formed a relationship with bacteria that are capable of "reformatting" atmospheric nitrogen into a substance that the plants can't live without.

Most of the prairie's nitrogen-fixing plants are members of the legume family, the familiar tribe of peas and beans. The nitrogen-fixing bacteria enter the legume root hairs while the plants are still in the seedling stage. Once established, the host plant produces root nodules to house the bacteria and their enzymes. Over time, each plant returns a certain amount of nutrients in an effort to sustain the symbiotic nitrogen-fixing partners living in association with its roots. The trade-off ensures that the plants will have an ample amount of available, usable nitrogen. Other plant forms, including blue-green algae, convert some atmospheric nitrogen. But by and large it's the legume tribe—native prairie plants like leadplant and scurf peas, wild indigos, wild alfalfas, and milk vetches—that does the bulk of nitrogen conversion.

Reichman's book reveals that ongoing research from experimental stations like Konza shows that an acre of native lowland prairie may contain hundreds of various forbs, legumes, and grasses, providing a dense ground cover and forming a nearly indivisible bond as long as rain falls and farmers and their tractors remain elsewhere. But that's only the prairie that meets the eye—below ground, a single pinch of prairie soil can contain several million bacteria cells. These bacteria are capable of retreating into soil cysts and spores when conditions aren't particularly favorable, then exploding into prominence when soils warm and the rains return. Under good conditions, a single acre of prairie soil may contain up to 5,000 pounds of bacteria.

Unplowed tallgrass prairie soil is a rich organic pudding. And while the amount of bacteria present staggers the imagination, it isn't even close to the amount of fungi. Plus there are algae, simple plants that require sunlight for photosynthesis, residing near the soil's surface, while single-celled animals like protozoans crowd the upper few inches of the soil profile.

At the same time, the prairie's upper crust literally crawls with minuscule animal life. You'll find the nematodes, both free-living and parasitic roundworms not much bigger than a single particle of soil. Some types of nematodes may number 5,000 per square foot within the upper eight inches of prairie earth. Most nematodes munch on fungi, while others are parasitic. Females lay eggs, and the young that hatch go through larval stages.

Larger yet are the centipedes and millipedes, beetle and fly larvae, cicada nymphs, mites, springtails, earthworms, and others from among the underground zoo that can actually outweigh, in pounds per acre, life forms that exist above the soil. Together these soil dwellers constitute the organic soup that makes tallgrass prairie hum with life.

Today most of this balanced and self-nurturing system has been ripped up and replaced with row crops, a monoculture of annual plants that only make withdrawals and never put nutrients back in the bank. It's an endeavor that eventually leads to a biological dead end, an endeavor dependent upon the use of carbon-based fertilizers, chemicals that feed yet never truly nourish. Fortunately, research at institutions like Konza Prairie results in scientific data that essentially reaffirm the obvious—most ecological associations like those that evolved over tens of thousands of years are too intricately intertwined for us to unravel at a whim and still expect long-term land health.

THE GRASSLAND LEGACY OF J. E. WEAVER

He never achieved the lasting fame of conservationists like Aldo Leopold or Theodore Roosevelt, but to his credit no man before or since has known the North American grasslands like John Ernest Weaver. The words he wrote about the prairie were wrung from the sweat of learning about grassland ecology from the roots up—literally. Weaver was an academic who understood that the science he sought to master required hands-on investigation, and that the data he collected over the years were best disseminated in a conversational manner that readers could both learn from and appreciate. He wrote a number of papers and several books about grasslands that remain timeless in both scope and energy—a fitting legacy for a man who dug miles of trenches related to his work, all while wearing a three-piece suit.

Weaver was born in Iowa in 1884, a prairie state that was already seeing its sod turned upside down as the region's rich black soils were fast becoming America's agricultural epicenter. He earned his doctorate at the University of Minnesota, taught botany at Washington State College, and accepted a position at the University of Nebraska in 1915. The Nebraska prairies would become his laboratory, classroom, and spiritual home for the rest of his professional lifetime. He remained at the university as a professor of plant ecology from 1917 until 1952, assembling material for books that included *Native Vegetation of Nebraska* and his unparalleled *Prairie Plants and Their Environment: A Fifty-Year Study in the Midwest.*

Weaver was obsessed with learning about prairie plants from the top of each flowering stem to the tip of the tiniest and deepest rootlet. To accomplish this, he and his students dug trenches, many of them fifteen feet deep, to reveal the roots of the prairie plants he was researching. Next, he'd carefully expose each individual root mass and then draw it in intricate detail.

Needless to say, few scientists have had the patience or the desire to duplicate such effort. In his day, no one understood the complexity of the underground prairie the way that J. E. Weaver did. Weaver undertook all these years of exhausting labor because he felt that to know grasslands, you have to become as one with the soil and the root systems that support all the endless miles of waving green leaves and stems. He understood that the engine driving a robust prairie was hidden underground.

In *Prairie Plants and Their Environment*, Weaver explained that frequently half—and often considerably more than half—of every grassland plant is invisible. For much of the year, the entirety of the living prairie is underground. The explosion of leaves and stems during the growing season is essentially refueling, exposing leaf surface to sunshine to funnel nutrients underground through the process of photosynthesis. For plants that are adequately nourished, the green season ends with a stem rapidly extending skyward, topped by tiny flowers and eventually seeds. Then nutrients migrate back to the roots to await another hot, humid, and hopefully rainy year of photosynthesis under the sun.

Weaver's trenches uncovered roots that mined much deeper than anyone had previously imagined. The professor discovered that the common prairie forb false boneset, a tall, coarse, not so colorful plant aboveground, waves in the wind atop a root system reaching sixteen feet deep or deeper. Another autumn prairie favorite, the truly colorful purple-flowering *Liatris* species, enriches the landscape on a flowering stem rarely more than several feet tall.

Weaver uncovered the underground growth of *Liatris* plants that also dug down sixteen feet, mining moisture and nutrients from every available prairie particle and pore. One of the plants the botany professor excavated was thirty-five years old. Weaver felt that native prairie plants evolved a long life in order to successfully develop the extensive root systems needed to mine nutrients and moisture at multiple levels. Vast root networks also allowed the plants to interact benignly with neighboring plants, sharing the chemical resources needed to prosper within a few square yards of subterranean prairie earth.

A contemporary gardening blogger who writes under the moniker Garden History Girl described Weaver's detailed drawings of root systems as nothing less than art. Certainly the perspective needed to portray these intricate and complicated systems in three-dimensional renderings sprang from a mind that seemed able to crawl into the soil and observe its surroundings from the viewpoint of some organic particle that just happened to be interacting with a rootlet. Weaver's fascination with prairie soil led to the knowledge that what we take for granted as a solid is, in fact, nearly as much air and water as dirt.

For example, Weaver found that the top one foot of little bluestem sod was only 43 to 50 percent solid matter. The remainder was pore space, about half of the space containing air, the rest water. A bottom-land patch of big bluestem grass was only 40 to 50 percent solid soil matter at seven feet deep, but at this depth the amount of available air had shrunk to 10 percent.

Weaver's research prairies were, in many ways, similar to Flint Hills vegetation, especially in the preponderance of bluestem grasses. Big and little bluestem comprised as much as 70 percent of the Nebraska vegetation he studied. The professor discovered that big bluestem, in its first season of growth, could put down roots from two to four feet deep, relying on the sunlight-intercepting ability of leaves spreading from stems as long as eighteen inches. In Nebraska, under good growing conditions, an established big bluestem plant can grow fourteen inches tall by June 1 and two and a half to three feet tall by July 1 and send up flower stalks topping out at seven to ten feet by the first of September.

Similar research indicated that Indiangrass, a plant of pale blue leaves and stems topped in autumn by a golden pyramid of seeds, tends to be much like big bluestem in habitat requirements and growth rates. Seeds of both big bluestem and Indiangrass have long, twisted awns that literally screw the seeds into the earth as they coil and uncoil with changes in humidity.

Little bluestem dominated much of Weaver's uplands, just as it does in the southern tallgrass country. Adapted to thinner, drier soils, this grass mines for water with extremely fine well-branched roots. Growth above the soil averages around fifteen inches or more depending upon rainfall, while the root system reaches down some five feet and spreads some twelve to eighteen inches. Soil moisture content is less on hilltops and slopes, so little bluestem's wider root system does an excellent job of absorbing any water that's available. Both big and little bluestem are long-lived plants, reproducing sometimes by wind-borne seeds but mostly by putting up shoots from subsoil rhizomes branching from the roots.

Little bluestem flower stalks are in place and abundant by late August. And while they average around eighteen inches long, when rainfall is sufficient the stalks may approach three feet. As the seeds mature into late fall, they take on a silvery cast that reminded some early botanists of an old man's beard, thus the scientific name *Andro*(man)*pogon*(beard).

Few grasses are more beautiful following a frost than little bluestem. Stems and leaves turn a coppery red that can look almost pink in a certain light, with the stems topped by abundant seeds, each seemingly spun from silver thread and quick to catch the intensity of autumn's angled sunlight. I've heard Cheyenne Indians refer to little bluestem as red grass. It follows the growing season, when leaves and stems are leached of their nutrients and serve as little more than a plant stand for whatever seeds the winds haven't dispersed. But in midsummer, as little bluestem pushes toward peak maturity, its overall tint can seem the reflection of a pale blue sky. That's the color of royalty on a prairie surging to combine spring rains, riotous sunlight, and dark organic soils into a matrix of roots, rootlets, fungi, insects, and microscopic plants, animals, and parasitic associates. From this rich soup spring tall stems with angled leaves that ride the wind in arched gracefulness and, with luck, may outlive many of us who benefit from their fecundity.

The tallgrass prairie has often been referred to as a sea of grass, an appropriate metaphor when you consider that the geologic history of the Flint and Osage Hills is based upon the ebb and flow of oceans. For millions of years, the region alternated between inundation by shallow marine seas and reemergence above sea level. Today's thick limestone beds are a result of eons of limey secretions and the skeletons of ancient saltwater flora and fauna that, cemented together, make up the fossil-rich strata that outcrop throughout these rolling hills.

Permian layers of limestone exposed in the Flint Hills approach a thickness of two hundred feet, with some estimated to be between 240 and 290 million years old. Even so, the region is considered ecologically young and still a borrower of plants and animals from neighboring systems. Modern prairie, still in the process of developing its own endemics, may manage to do so in a few thousand years if we can manage to protect the small amount of tall grassland left.

While trees are generally revered worldwide, grasses get little appreciation. Not many realize that our native grasses are an advanced group of specialized plants with a remarkable ability to adapt to the forces that shaped them. Tallgrass prairie grasses evolved under pressures exerted by some formidable opponents—fire, drought, and the appetites of large and small grazers ranging from bison to grasshoppers.

The give-and-take between grasses and grazers has been beneficial to both. Over time, grasses added silica content both to shore up their vertical stature and to deter the animals that would eat them. In turn, grass consumers responded by evolving high-crowned, wear-resistant teeth to counter the added grit in the prairie salads they savored. Native grasses battled back against close cropping by consumers like bison by developing rapid spurts of growth both upward and laterally and by producing new shoots that formed along horizontal underground stems. Native grasses also became capable of renewing growth at any point along the stem.

Therefore, if a cow crops a grass plant six inches from the ground, that plant will once again start growing from that six-inch point. Cut a tree trunk and what you have left is a stump. Renewed growth may appear in the form of suckers or runners, but the stump remains a stump. Grasses produce new growth from meristems, actively dividing cells located throughout the stem that enable the plant to telescope upward rather than laterally, with new leaf mass being added throughout the process.

Obviously, native grasses are tough and resilient. Yet even the toughest can be damaged beyond repair by overgrazing. Grasses continually gnawed to the ground can't produce enough leaf surface for adequate photosynthesis. Over time, the roots of continually close-cropped grasses lose their vigor, start to decline, and are replaced by annual grasses and forbs of lower palatability and nutritional value.

Land managers then attack these "weeds" with expensive herbicides when they could have alleviated the problem by simply allowing their grasses a little extra growth. Prairie grasses can bounce back if grazing is deferred so that the plants can recuperate and rejuvenate leafy surface area. Historically, buffalo herds cropped the grasses closely and then moved on while the prairie repaired itself and regained vitality. Today, ranchers too often disregard grassland's need for rest and, over time, watch their acreage degenerate into stands of invasive annuals from Europe and Asia, along with woody invaders that barely provide fodder for grasshoppers.

We don't often think of plants as being mindful of their own long-term needs and biological challenges, but studies have shown that tallgrass prairie grasses are exactly that. According to prairie ecologist J. E.

Weaver, native grasses seem to understand that the energy and nutrients they absorb during a good growing year are a luxury, so when times are good they allocate a little extra to extend a flowering stem skyward and engage in the manufacture of more seed. Yet most of the time, when the growing season is average or less than average, grass plants bypass any allocation of reserve energy to seed production.

Reporting on a study conducted at Konza Prairie, O. J. Reichman said that researchers looking at native grass seed generation over a period of ten years found that less than 5 percent of the study area's big bluestem plants produced seed in any one year. During the best year, one of adequate rainfall and sunlight, some 30 percent of the plants flowered.

Seeds are expensive in terms of the energy and nutrients needed to make them, and they aren't terribly efficient when it comes to developing into new plants and passing along the parent plants' genetic potential. Perennial grasses have, over time, discovered a better way: they turn to their underground resources, those rhizomes extending out horizontally from the central root mass. Prairie grass rhizomes are able to form buds in autumn and begin new growth in spring. These young clones can draw upon the resources stored in the roots of the parent plant, while seeds can draw only upon the minimal energy provided within the seed package itself.

It's understandable then, why true native prairie is mostly an underground extension of ropy roots and rhizomes. By investing in a complex underground system, prairie plants and forbs have survived for decades upon end, withstanding finicky rainfall patterns, rapacious insects, and the wanderlust of bygone buffalo herds.

In a healthy prairie, carbon is king. It's the carbon in the air that prairie plants are after, and as they breathe they expel oxygen just as we expel carbon dioxide following each deep breath. Photosynthesis is what we call the process that reconfigures the carbon into the glucose and other sugars required for plant growth and overall prosperity, just as the oxygen released into the atmosphere by plants fuels human growth and prosperity. It's a successful association, resulting in success for a wide array of plants and the billions of people who can't survive without them. Native grasslands also utilize carbon that would otherwise infiltrate the atmosphere and contribute to the climate change that is affecting our oceans, our weather patterns, our seasons, and in general life here on earth.

Prairie plants provide for their food by collecting the electromagnetic energy we call sunlight and, through processes initiated by refined cells in the leaves, converting it into biological energy. According to my old biology textbooks, this chemical process takes place in leaf cells called chloroplasts, which contain pigments including chlorophyll. Microscopic openings in the leaves, the stomata, open to take in air. Plants withdraw the carbon, oxygen gets expelled, and eventually the carbon molecules provide the sugars and starches needed to sustain life. At the same time, the roots of each prairie plant soak up the water and minerals needed to complete this nourishing chemistry that began as simple sunlight and air. Historically, the results have been a healthy plant and a healthy planet.

Botanists are continually isolating the methods that prairie plants utilize to provide for their own success, including how carbon interacts with available sunlight to instigate growth. Plants, like people, are always looking for a time and a place to excel. Over thousands of years, a complex community of prairie plants evolved various chemical configurations that allowed some to photosynthesize in cooler weather while others grew best as the sun climbed toward its midsummer zenith. As a result, we have grasses that complete their carbon or growth cycle during late winter and early spring, followed by grasses that begin the bulk of their growth as these cool-season grasses flower and prepare to go dormant. Essentially, as my college professors pointed out, a healthy native prairie can and will provide the robust greenery required for successful life on earth practically throughout the year.

A biologically thriving prairie, as plant ecologist J. E. Weaver described it, contains two hundred or more species of native plants per square mile, all of them locked in a struggle to exist. Each plant faces a contest for light, water, and soil nutrients, essentials eagerly sought by numerous competitors. Weaver's observations confirmed that while plants may be damaged by threats ranging from overgrazing to drought to late-season frosts, few mature, established plants are ever actually killed.

Weaver was convinced that these complex grassland systems continue to exist through a sort of evolved alliance. Individual plants share the soil at various levels, obtain sunlight at varying heights, and make their maximum demands for light, water, and nutrients at different times during the year. He saw this symbiosis at work in the way that native legumes add nitrogen to the soil, taller plants provide shade for lower ones, mat-forming plants reduce water runoff, and sunlight inevitably reaches individual plants at a variety of levels. Weaver found that, compared to cropland, native prairies had far fewer fluctuations in soil and air temperatures, maintained humidity at a consistently higher level, and experienced less evaporation.

It's just basic biology that plants, like every other living thing, are engaged in a near-constant search for nutrition. Most of us don't require a lecture to understand that humans lining up in front of a community soup kitchen are hoping to meet at least a portion of their daily nutritional needs. Prairie plants, on the other hand, search for nourishment mostly out of sight and mind since much of the mechanism involved in providing that nourishment is sequestered underground. Even so, Weaver grasped that a plant's methods for obtaining nourishment are remarkably similar to many of our own as we work to appease our hunger and make our genes available to future generations.

University of Alberta experimental plant ecologist J. C. Cahill, appearing on public television's *Nature* series in April 2013, described how a dodder seedling (an orange vinelike parasite found on native prairie) has but seventy-two hours to locate a host plant. Otherwise it dies. Dodder has a strong preference for certain species, and the tendrils that attach themselves to these favorites use chemistry to sniff out the plants that allow for successful growth. For dodder, second best isn't an option when better choices are close at hand.

The *Nature* special, "What Plants Talk About," showed that when selecting a host plant, these dodder tendrils writhe about in the air, seeking the chemical signature of the host they're searching for. The host plants emit a distinctive chemical odor when they breathe, and the parasitic dodder vine is evolutionarily programmed to know which ones best fulfill its needs.

Modern scientific conjecture has it that other plants may communicate in a similar chemical language and also indulge in animal-like behavior when threatened. During the TV special, Cahill explained how ongoing research is toying with the hypothesis that plants invaded by pests issue a chemical scream that may summon insects that like to dine on the attackers. At the same time, this silent scream may serve as a warning to other plants, urging them to erect chemical defenses to deter the coming insect onslaught. It's amazing what you can learn from TV if you give up sitcoms, blood, and gore for just a single night and tune in to PBS.

Cahill described another theory gaining acceptance among botanists. Insect pest saliva has a chemical component that plants learn to recognize. Some plants can switch pollinators when the offspring of these pollinators—like the caterpillars emerging from the eggs that certain pollinating moths lay—start to do too much physical damage. Therefore, some botanists believe that plants may change their chemical voice to summon a different pollinator, or change the shape of their flowers, or even change the time of their flowering. Some may literally switch pollinators from, say, a hawk moth to a hummingbird. If as some visionary researchers suggest, this marvelous bioengineering can happen within a matter of days, then it may be that we're not as far removed from the prairie world as we think. Even more intriguing is the hypothesis that neighboring plants can eavesdrop on these changes and start making adjustments of their own.

On the northern plains, alien invaders like certain knapweeds have declared war against the natives. They attack with toxins emanating from their roots, intent upon overwhelming native species and creating an aggressive knapweed community. According to the U.S. Department of Agriculture, researchers at Colorado State University have discovered that native lupines produce a chemical that not only repels the foreigners but spreads to protect neighboring native species as well. In the end, it was a simple little legume not particularly favored by ranchers that stuck to its roots in an effort to protect the homeland.

The PBS special "What Plants Talk About" featuring dodder tentacles writhing about in search of a host plant also featured footage showing that sibling plants tend to share root space, and that plants with similar genetics seem to do a better job of sharing nutrients. Trees, according to the program hosts, pass nutrients along to their seedling offspring. Such family traits are tied to the interconnectedness of the fungal networks linking these vast underground systems.

Biology 101 explains that a fungus by itself can't produce its own food—it's up to each plant to make a donation of carbon-based sugars. Leaves of grass construct the carbon molecules that become glucose, the basic building block of life on earth. Plant-produced glucose can become carbohydrates, including sucrose, lactose, ribose, cellulose, and certain starches. If plant materials containing these sugars are eaten, they are then available for conversion to fats, oils, amino acids, and proteins.

So what's out of sight in a prairie can't be kept out of mind if you're the least bit interested in what makes a grassland one of the most complicated and successful ecosystems on the planet. A professor friend of mine, Albert Blair, once told me that a single acre of underground prairie might contain enough vertebrate and invertebrate life to equal the weight of ten horses. All I know is that when my father hitched up a team to plow our garden overlooking the headwaters of Sycamore

Fuel for a Fiery Green Engine

Creek, the soil gleamed blue-black in the sunlight. The fragrance was that of life itself, and you could feel the complexity and organic wholeness in a handful of dirt.

Our little tract of prairie earth grew wonderful food, including huge ears of corn, countless peas and beans, fat potatoes and onions, and robust orange carrots that our horses savored like candy. Tomatoes were red as a prairie sunrise and not only delicious but nutrient rich, flavored by composting plant material, cow manure, and around thirty-six inches of rainfall every year. Today, when prepackaged vegetables taste much like the packages themselves, my memories of that garden and the rich dark soil that grew all those delicious meals border on the sublime.

SPRING'S FIRST WARM RAIN

Yesterday afternoon, the first true spring rain began to fall, warm and gentle, deep into the night. Only ten days before, the grass was weighted down by sleet, then light snow. But yesterday's rain was different. It helped amphibians find their voices, allowed leopard frogs to serenade the lakes and ponds with a raspy snore and chuckle. I saw Carolina chickadees checking out a cavity in an aging redbud tree, and eastern bluebirds grew talkative, their calls soft and nasal.

This morning out in the tallgrass, on a limestone ridge overlooking the old city lake west of Pawhuska, a mature bald eagle was perched atop a post oak tree, a tall and spreading oak growing directly from exposed bedrock. It's a stately tree and a fit perch for such a regal bird. And since the eagle has remained south well into the nesting season, it's most likely a resident with a mate and a nest nearby. I haven't seen the nest, but I've seen these eagles feeding on white-tailed deer carrion. Road-killed venison, ubiquitous these days in the southern tallgrass country, provides a fitting meal for birds that like their protein in superlarge quantities.

On the lake ring-necked ducks, a flock of migrants caught up in this season of restless movement, skim over the surface as they dig deeply with wings and webbed feet at air and water, laboring to get airborne. A bedraggled coyote, gaunt and frayed here at the intersection of winter and spring, dashes toward the upper end of the lake, leery of the peaceful approach of my pickup truck. Often these younger animals can't overcome the power of coyote curiosity, and they slow down to look over their shoulder or even stop for a defining glance. Not this young song dog. It's headed for cover as if I'm part of a sheriff's posse and it's a cattle thief—a scenario that may be more than fantasy, considering that the surrounding pastures are dotted with newborn calves.

Calving season is a time of vulnerability. Cattle sense it, coyotes know it, even the eagle in the treetop understands that scavenged beef may soon be on the menu. These thoughts are made tangible when, at the top of a draw that spills a trickle of springwater into the lake, a slight movement betrays a very young Black Angus calf.

The longer I stare, the more the recently born youngster twitches nervously. However, it's reluctant to leave the bloated carcass of its mother, now stiffened by rigor mortis with legs pointing skyward. The scene is a sad one, and I can only surmise that the cow died following the birth of the calf, and that this newborn grasps little other than to stay close to the first living creature it encountered following the womb. Hopefully, the rancher will soon discover that a cow is missing and search for her. But the timbered draw is deep and time favors four-legged investigators. More than likely, the calf will die before it is found and coyote and eagle will feast.

March 14, the day of this year's first warm rain, could just as easily have been a day of deep snow or one of bitter north winds and bare limbs sheathed in ice. March is a schizoid season here on the prairie. But this morning the temperature is in the mid-fifties climbing toward a high in the seventies. There's a crisp north wind, enough to create a bit of a wind chill on the higher prairie to the north, but here below the limestone-rimmed cuestas the weather's almost balmy.

The protruding limestone cap, perched atop the sloping hills like a metal roof on a grassy earthen lodge, is bluish gray, cracked and layered by years of weathering. Freezing, thawing, the hydraulic manipulation of tree roots, the steady dissolution of calcareous rock due to acidic rainfall: all have worked to sculpt this layer of stone made up of skeletons and secretions of ancient ocean creatures. Already small dark green leaves pressed against gray stone mark where stems of wild currants will soon erupt with long golden trumpet-shaped flowers, an early spring bouquet contrasting with the stark rock outcropping.

In places limestone islands have eroded away from the parent rock, leaving grass-encircled mounds of stone, some six feet or more in height and as big around as a tractor tire. These mounds seem to be where the wild currants grow best, and in a few weeks the artistic presentation will be complete—blue-gray rock draped with wildflowers streaked with bright yellow and crimson, all merging at the time when dark purple violets begin to flower beneath limestone ledges.

On a warm day, any snakes with dens deep in the limestone outcrop will slip outside to bask and contemplate the move from denning to foraging territory. Pack rats will return to the shallow depressions in the bedrock they've chosen as latrines, to ponder pack rat business and consider the appetites of the timber rattlesnakes soon to wait motionless beside the complexity of mouse and rat trails stitched throughout the tallgrass. And in a few days, wild turkey toms will begin to strut in the bottomland timber, their rattling gobbles cutting through mist and fog with the resonance of an amplified sports announcer.

This morning an e-mail from a bird-watcher living some sixty miles to the south said that American golden-plovers were foraging on the turf at a city sod farm. It's a formal announcement that the South American migrants are back on this continent. In the 1870s, when the Osages first settled on their reservation here, winged visitors from South America would have darkened the sky as they passed over these prairies. Market hunting and habitat alteration put an end to that spectacle, but fortunately a few greater prairie-chickens remain to exhale their breathy, far-carrying cooing in an effort to woo feathered lady friends and remind us that our prairies are more than just cows, hay, and blank space between fences.

March's maddening summons beckons snakes from dens, birds from sister continents, and a surge of hormones in creatures large and small. At the edge of the tallgrass, where prairie creeks empty into the broad Arkansas River, silver-sided fish ease into the flow, ready to swim up shallow, narrow streams and release their eggs to the care of the current. Overwintering insects grow active on warm days, focused on jump-starting the next generation.

Several mornings ago, a massive flight of snow geese split the sky overhead, the energy in their calling indicating that this was more than just another flight to feed. Lengthening daylight insisted that, no matter what the weather, life's compass now pointed steadily north, and the geese were bound for distant horizons. Later I thought I saw a

Spring's First Warm Rain

smaller flock flying low over a lake. Yet it seemed that these birds were bigger, their voices deeper, less shrill. After a few seconds, I realized that the birds were trumpeter swans, once common but now another of the prairie voices that have grown dim over the years.

Best of all, maybe, were the antics of the buffalo on the Nature Conservancy's Tallgrass Prairie Preserve. From a nucleus of some 300 animals released upon the 39,000-plus-acre tract in 1993, the herd has grown closer to 3,000. On this particular March afternoon, buffalo cows and their soon-to-be yearling calves were grazing across patches of prairie burned last autumn. The burns held a hint of new green grass, and the bison were eager to nibble at it, moving steadily across the rolling landscape, disregarding all but this tender treasure underfoot.

A mile away I came across a band of brothers, half a dozen bison bulls in their prime. Rather than pick daintily at the new spring growth on the burns, the boys were hanging out in the tall bleached stalks of last autumn's growth. Some grazed on grasses cured on the stem, others probably found green shoots penetrating the basal clumps of dormant bunchgrasses. But mostly they seemed indifferent to anything other than a lifestyle of lounging, saving their strength for summer and the rut, for the battles their genetics prepared them to fight, for the raucous, roaring, dirt-flying, bone-battering wars that would determine which genes would dominate in next spring's calf crop and which would wait their turn.

Nearly 3,000 animals is enough to get just a glimpse, yet a small one at that, of what Native Americans witnessed on buffalo hunts during centuries past. You truly need thousands of buffalo, roaming freely on tens of thousands of unfenced acres, just to catch a fragment of the spectacle. I can't pretend to imagine the excitement of the explorers who wrote about seeing millions of buffalo spread out over miles of undulating grassland.

Journalists of the early 1800s, from George Catlin to Colonel Richard Irving Dodge, remarked about many of the same things you notice here. One is the restlessness of the buffalo when they graze. It's as if some invisible force is always tugging at them. This compulsion to be on the move may be a trait left over from a time before fences, when the herd drifted, mixed, and mingled across the landscape, grazing the grasses hard and then leaving them to recover. Predators and scavengers followed this huge, revolving, restless mass of life and in doing so helped the herd create its own ecology, its own earthly universe as it went about the business of borrowing energy from sunlight through the consumption of grass.

By afternoon the north wind has subsided somewhat, yet northern harriers continue their twisting and tumbling on the wing. The harriers are superb low-altitude fliers, able to overcome all the bursts and kinks of a stout prairie wind and still concentrate on the rats and mice they come upon by sailing quietly only inches above the tallgrass. After stopping to watch the harriers hunt, I turn to discover that the last of the buffalo are easing over a distant hill and will soon be gone from sight. As it is, the spun gold of winter hair atop their disappearing humps glistens in the strengthening sunlight.

A few of the cows, giving in to the joy of new spring grass and the crisp prodding of the March wind, begin to gallop and buck like colts in some Kentucky bluegrass horse pasture. One leaps as high as the hood of my pickup truck, then takes off at a full gallop, headed for a band of cows a quarter mile distant. The speed the cow achieves is startling, considering the ungainly outline of the animal, and there's nothing to do but wish her Godspeed. This is the largest expanse of protected tallgrass prairie left in the world, and hers is a rightful place within it.

A prairie hay meadow, shorn nearly as short as a suburban lawn in early July and then allowed to rest a year before the next annual shearing, is a wonderful place to watch the increasing stature of wildflowers as spring progresses. These meadows are rarely grazed and have but a single job to do—grow as much plant life as the sun and the rain allow and, in doing so, provide a dense carpet of native grasses, forbs, and legumes to be turned into cattle fodder at a time when the plants are at their leafiest.

Investment in a hay meadow is nil. All that's required to grow native grass is an adequately wet spring. The rancher supplies tractor, mowing machine, and bailer while being spared the expense of fertilizer, herbicide, and seed plus the time and equipment required for tilling and planting. The result of allowing nature to do the work is nutritious hay from acres rich in highly palatable native plant species that often disappear from neighboring pastures with their resident cows. Hay meadows never suffer from selective grazing targeting the more nutritious plants or from uniform overgrazing. Native grass hay fields endure a day or more's worth of indignity, and then the mechanized invaders are gone.

Following this quick annual haircut, the meadow returns to doing what it does best. During the growing season, prairie hay meadows provide for birds, butterflies, countless insects, small mammals, reptiles, and all those that eat and in turn are eaten in an endlessly revolving and evolving process. The meadows accomplish this by absorbing sunlight and rainfall to enable photosynthesis that produces nutrients stored in roots and rhizomes. All this stored energy in turn anchors the circular ebb and flow of perennial plant life. When lengthening daylight awakens the life force in prairie plants following several months of dormancy, the release of energy to grow leaf, stem, flower, and seed not only invigorates bird, mammal, reptile, and amphibian but also those of us who are as renewed by the arrival of spring as much as any frog, toad, or salamander.

This morning a bright Easter Sunday reaches for a high in the mid-seventies. Big dollops of white clouds drift across a sky the color of turquoise. Below, the previously blank green canvas of a prairie hay meadow now appears to be the aftermath of some divine domestic dispute. Flakes of blue mirroring the color of the sky are scattered across the meadow, and it seems that some of the Greek gods of old, the ones with decidedly human foibles, have been chipping away at the heavens. The result is abstractly beautiful, a rich checkerboard of blue and green that actually harmonizes in a manner that's difficult to comprehend—until you see it in person on a spring morning when the light is still strongly angular and the atmosphere clean and fresh.

Close up, the flecks of fallen sky prove to be one of a tallgrass prairie spring's most beautiful flowers. Common names include prairie pleatleaf and celestial lily. Yet a lily this flower is not. *Nemastylis geminiflora* is a member of the iris family. The flower grows from a typical iris-like bulb, and the rich blue inflorescence with bright yellow anthers offers only a fleeting display of floral beauty, yet one that's difficult to forget.

Nemastylis opens late in the morning and closes before three in the afternoon, sunshine or not. Essentially, the plant waits until the day is warm enough for insects to be active, then closes as the peak pollinating period subsides. And even though each flower seems faultlessly engineered, its life span is but a single day. Following pollination and the production of ripened seed, the plant disappears until the following spring. Subsequently, the work involved in remaining a wild iris continues underground. Prairie pleatleaf is prone to colonize, a fact of life evidenced in this turquoise-flecked hay meadow on an April day, at a time when native grassland is striving to ignite the green flame of another growing season.

Easter sunrise services for a pair of coachwhip snakes appear to be on hold as they wait for the morning to warm a little. The snakes display torpid indifference to my presence as the sun strives to heat the exposed bedrock overlooking Hominy Creek. The snakes are shiny black except for reddish brown tails. The scale pattern is striking and looks like plaited leather, thus the common name coachwhip. Coachwhips here in the tallgrass country generally are dark, while western varieties often are a lighter shade of brown. Generally the braided leather scale pattern provides a better field mark than color does.

Below the hay meadow, the headwaters of Hominy Creek are murky from a series of thunderstorms. The brown-stained water reflects varying shades of green inherent in new leaves on streamside trees— the deeply lobed and pointed leaves of Shumard oak, the serrated leaves of chinquapin oak, and the rounded lobes of bur oak. Down by the water's edge, a diamondback water snake remains motionless yet observant, coiled in its favorite hangout, a tangle of buttonbush roots. Equally unmoved is a rough green snake, two feet long or more, stretched out along a branch growing from a sapling redbud tree. The snake's skin, nearly a perfect match for the color of the new leaves that surround it, seems excellent camouflage as I ease up to photograph the taciturn reptile. It's not until I concentrate on focusing the macro lens that the snake's twin suddenly materializes out of the leaf patterns. In fact, there are *two* rough green snakes sharing the small tree, and their proximity implies that spring for rough green snakes is also in the air, maybe even a little romance.

Another reptile, taking the sun atop a sandstone boulder along the ridge overlooking the creek, makes little effort to blend in with the background. A male eastern collared lizard, maybe a foot long from tip of snout to tip of tail, displays the bright blue-green coloration of the breeding season. And although he seems lethargic, this is a lizard that, energized by a sunny spring morning, can get up on his hind legs and make tracks with amazing speed. The sight of a big lizard, running upright, is more than just a little unnerving, enough so that I've seen several big tough men bolt for cover.

Easter can't be complete without bird activity striving toward a spring breeding-season crescendo. Today the trees are churning with the hyperbusy insect gleaning of blue-gray gnatcatchers, warbler-size birds that look somewhat like shrunken mockingbirds. They search, scour, and scold like miniature harridans, their activity nonstop. Overhead, one of the stream's more regal residents screams to its mate with a distinctly keening, petulant tone. These red-shouldered hawks are deep into the breeding season. Finely streaked red and white breasts distinguish the species, but to me the most poignant field mark is their powerful, beseeching vocals while on the wing at breeding time.

Downstream, from somewhere deep in the shadows, another very vocal species does its best to bring your neck hairs to attention. Barred owls are talking, and while the typical "who cooks for you all" phrasing seems especially supercharged this morning, it's the scream, much like what you'd expect from an actress being attacked in a horror movie, that actually *does* make your hair stand up a little.

Recent showers have left water standing in ephemeral pools, and even though this Easter arrives early in the month, we've had frog conversation for more than a week now. Tiny Blanchard's cricket frogs, their calls like striking two small stones together, have been active along shallow streams. Later in the year, when the weather warms, they'll turn tan and brown. But these early Easter amphibians are presently almost black, eager to absorb every particle of energy the sun can provide.

Scissor-tailed flycatchers are back from wintering in Mexico and Central America, ready once again to lord their subtle beauty and spectacular aerodynamics over the tallgrass country. Male scissortails, regal in shades of silver, gray, black, and orange, possess extremely long tails. Mature males may be fourteen or fifteen inches long, half or more of that being tail feathers.

Scissortails look much their kingbird kin, except for the tail. Females and juvenile birds aren't as endowed as the older roosters, which are unmistakable as they perch out on the prairie ready for an insect to fly past. When the chase begins, the long tail separates into a lengthy V, allowing the bird to twist and turn in flight with unbelievable agility. Today, like his handsome yet pugnacious cousin the eastern kingbird, a resident scissortail is testing his flight feathers and aerodynamic adroitness by picking on a crow that mistakenly flew too close to the elegant bully. The big rooster scissortail immediately pursues and, with aerial dynamics that would make a fighter pilot proud, proceeds to pluck at the fleeing crow's tail feathers. When it comes to maneuverability, the crow places a distant second in a contest with a scissortail. Therefore, the black marauder appears happy to flee the premises in a hurry, rather than hang around and search for scissortail eggs or nestlings.

Downslope from where the scissortail perches as he surveys his spring and summer kingdom, a three-toed box turtle lumbers along, easing through the fresh white flowers of wild strawberries pressed against newly green grasses. The turtle's smooth brown shell contrasts with its pinkish orange facial markings. This young male's face is painted like an Osage ready for the warpath, although war is not an issue for this wanderer. He appears to be around ten years old and more inclined toward romance. The season is ripe with reptile love in the air, inducing wanderlust and a sad assembly of crushed box turtles staining highway asphalt. Box turtles go about their business with single-minded purpose, yet speed and agility aren't part of their physical repertoire. Far too many end up as tidbits for scavengers. Fortunately, this guy has little other than protruding limestone and strawberry blossoms to contend with, and I'm certain that both of us have earmarked the spot for a sample of luscious wild fruit come May. Wild strawberries may be small, but their taste is inimitable. No commercially raised variety can compare.

April is the month of little flowers here in the tallgrass. They grow close to the ground and reproduce before the grasses spring up to dominate the landscape. The sloping hillside that serves as a stage for wild strawberries and adventuresome box turtles also nurtures low-growing purple violets with heart-shaped leaves, yellowish white false garlic, pinkish white spring beauties, brashly purple-pink verbena, bright yellow bladderpod, delicate blue-eyed grass, lavender wood sorrel, yellow and white fleabane, ground-hugging clusters of yellow parsley, and pale yellow puccoons. None is much more than five or six inches tall, and all will be but a memory by May, the month of the Little-Flower-Killer Moon, according to Osage historian John Joseph Mathews.

The day's Easter Sunday outdoor activities end at the Nature Conservancy's Tallgrass Prairie Preserve north of Pawhuska. The rolling landscape is green from recent prescribed burning, and thunderstorms have made mud baths of the preserve's buffalo wallows. As a result, many of the resident bison wear dried earthen armor as their Easter finery. Hawks are on the wing, and both redtails and harriers fly over the grassland carrying recently captured mice.

The northern harriers seem to dip and bob like the little balsa wood gliders we tossed around as kids, their flight purposeful, elegant, and low to the ground. On one stark black burn covering several hundred acres, a flock of Smith's longspurs gleans sustenance from what appears to be lifeless devastation. The birds, drab brown with buffy streaked breasts, walk, feed, then lift as one and fly a short distance to alight and begin to feed again. Upland sandpipers watch the proceedings from fence posts and, as the afternoon warms, dwarf American toads begin to trill from temporary pools, joining the birdlike chirping of Strecker's chorus frogs already in progress.

Before long, these blackened acres streaked with gray ash will be a carpet of emerald green grass electrified under the full strength of spring sunlight. Within weeks, reddish orange buffalo calves will be bucking and galloping across a landscape of undulating greenness, and the promise of renewal that underscores the Easter season will be fulfilled. Across oceans and continents, other cultures will make pilgrimages to holy places of great antiquity, while here at home in the tallgrass I'll be content with precocious buffalo calves, patches of tiny wildflowers, and the mystical vocals of prairie-chickens.

Each year around the end of April in the southern tallgrass, white flowers appear on the dark green foliage of blackberry vines. Often the blackberries flower after several days of warm, humid weather followed by a sharp cold front that brings with it a thunderstorm, then chilly north winds the next day. For a night or two temperatures dip into the low forties, sometimes the thirties, and country folk agree that we're in the grip of Blackberry Winter, a cold snap they'll testify to as an annual certainty, one that's happened throughout time on the day when the blackberries bloom.

My mother prepared for Blackberry Winter as a matter of course, and for years the phenomenon seemed factual. Finally it occurred to me that lingering cold fronts dip south frequently in late April, and that the occasion was mainly coincidence, this flowering of blackberries on a chilly day. Even the *Farmers' Almanac*, that forecaster of all things rural and weather-related, plays similar percentages. But for a kid, it's easier to put your trust in a mother's firm prediction: "The blackberries are flowering, go find your jackets." And so we did.

In April 2015, Blackberry Winter happened on the twentieth and lasted, off and on, for about a week. The north wind was oftentimes sharp, and the overnight lows dipped into the lower forties. The southern tallgrass hosted several fronts that resulted in overcast skies and cool rains. Even so, spring continued its irrepressible march toward May. Bird migrations flowed north, maybe slowed at times by the weather yet never fully impeded by fronts, cold winds, or sullen gray skies. Blackberry Winter tends to be not much more than a slight weather hiccup when it comes to interrupting the great spring growing-season surge.

Sometimes the weather moods can turn a bit freakish, and the prairies must bear up under late frosts and freezes. Snowflakes have fallen in late April, but lengthening daylight is incredibly quick at healing any damage done. Contingency plans are programmed into prairie plants and animals, allowing them to dig in for a day or two while winter suffers the season's final death throes. Auxiliary buds replace leaves singed by cold snaps. Insects conjure up body chemistry antifreeze that allows them to wait out the return of warmth. Occasionally frosts play havoc with flowering oak trees, and an autumn acorn crop may be reduced as a result.

The highly visible signature of Blackberry Winter is the number of conspicuous white flowers on prickly canes arching out of last year's tan grasses. In a couple of months the dark purple fruit, tart and sweet at the same time, will tempt berry picker and bird, coyote and box turtle, to partake of a seedy feast. In my childhood it was time to take galvanized metal buckets out into the grasslands and come home covered with bloody scratches, the buckets heavy with blackberries that would become cobbler the following Sunday. I don't know if many families even bother to bake pies these days, but the berries remain just as flavorful. Maybe the birds are thankful that so many country people have moved to the city, leaving more blackberries for harvesters on the wing.

On a morning in late April, with the sky slow to clear and the wind blowing sharply from the north, the blackberry canes, heavy with white flowers, were arched over to blend with newly green grasses exploding skyward in the pastures. Buffalo were on the move across the rolling hills of the Tallgrass Prairie Preserve. Cows, in bunches from fifty to a hundred or more, seemed restless.

I focused my binoculars on a small herd loafing on an unburned hillside more than a quarter mile away and quickly began to pick out the shorter orange objects nestled amid the waist-high brown stalks of last year's little bluestem. Within minutes one of the calves rose to nurse, and it became apparent that Blackberry Winter this year coincided with hundreds of bison calves born on the newly greening prairie.

Preserve personnel had set fire to the land in a patchwork pattern, leaving grazing meadows for the buffalo among taller nesting cover for eastern meadowlarks, upland sandpipers, northern bobwhite quail, and greater prairie-chickens, to name but a few of the many ground nesters that require clumps of last year's dried grasses for concealment. Buffalo bulls, content to loll around in groups of five or six, rested near the freshly burned prairie where they grazed. Most of the cows with new calves were in the taller vegetation. However, as the sky cleared in the afternoon, the cows moved out in a long line, heading for the burns and the tender green new growth soaking up sunlight and sprinkled with yellow and blue wildflowers.

By late in the afternoon, the line of cows marching over a prairie mound seemed like a scene from the heyday of Buffalo Bill. Hundreds of bison, many with young calves, were strung out over half a mile or more, and some of the calves, maybe just a few hours old, struggled with the pace. Cows at the back of the line stopped and waited patiently for the reddish orange youngsters to catch up. The last calf in line walked tentatively, its back somewhat arched, its gait unsteady. The mother cow, maybe twenty yards ahead, turned around and urged the new calf onward. It was obvious that she was eager to remain with the others, and the wobbly-legged newborn had little choice other than to toughen up and learn that to be a buffalo is to be a part of the herd, and that the social bond is almost as strong as a mother's need to care for her young.

Most of the buffalo and their calves were small brown dots in the distance when another cow galloped into view. She seemed agitated, bawled loudly, stopped for a moment, glanced back, then once again started after the others. This time, however, she was plainly distraught. The cow began to bounce, much like African antelope I've seen in nature films or like mule deer in flight. She continued this pogo stick gait for maybe twenty or thirty yards, then stopped and looked back in the direction she had come, almost bouncing in place, her agitation like an electric charge over the calm twilight grasslands.

I scanned the hillside that the herd had crossed, certain that a calf was somehow responsible for the cow's frantic activity. And there it was—a newborn, amid some of the taller brown grasses. The orange calf had managed to make it to its feet but seemed unsure what to do next.

By this time, the cow seemed emotionally ready to explode. She began the bouncing kangaroo gait again, this time back in the direction of her calf. When she came within approximately thirty yards of it she stopped and waited, glancing nervously at the calf, then back to the other cows steadily disappearing in the distance. Finally, after minutes that seemed like hours and with the mother cow almost imploring the calf to take a step, the newborn did manage a faltering stride, then another. The calf's advance was slow, woefully so, and I wondered if it had been injured at birth or was physically deficient in some way. The cow was so torn between her desire to stay with the others and the urge to stay with the calf that I thought this must be her first birth, and the role of motherhood as yet unclear.

One thing was clear as the calf took a few more hesitant steps in the cow's direction. The golden light of late evening was spilling over the emerald green expanse, and as the light diminished a coyote chorus came up from all directions, the sharp yipping interspersed with high-pitched barks urging the moon to follow the sun, informing the prairie that as the shadows deepened, coyote prowling would commence. If the distraught cow left the calf to join the other cows, then the newborn, only hours old from the look of it, would provide a feast for these lesser cousins of the buffalo wolves that once followed the herds.

Had this been 1815 rather than 2015, maybe wolves would have already killed the calf. Or maybe some of the older cows would have stayed with the nervous young cow had wolves been near. The wolf-buffalo dynamic is a saga of survival whose time has passed, still to be seen only in Yellowstone National Park and Wood Buffalo National Park in Canada. Even so, as the drama unfolded, I felt as if I was witnessing a scene straight out of pre-European America, with a few key players missing. The calf took another step in the direction of its mother and I eased away, allowing this crisis of young motherhood to achieve a more natural, uninterrupted ending.

Just before the bright orange burst of sunset, several upland sandpipers settled on the tall fence posts marking the preserve boundary. One cranked up the volume on the tribe's melodious liquid warble, while six young buffalo bulls arose from their resting places amid short green grass and began to graze. Before darkness spread over the rolling hills, a flock of brown-headed cowbirds descended upon the six bulls to search for insects around their feet.

Sundown's final gasp was spectacular. The green landscape bled into a rich red-orange atmosphere streaked with golden contrails. The bison seemed concerned with little other than the succulent forage underfoot. Their winter coats showed patches of chocolate brown bare skin, and the bulls paused mainly to scratch the itch of transformation. Patches of buffalo wool were scattered across the ground, a sign that winter was over, and that Blackberry Winter mattered little to a massive animal with so much nutritious food to eat.

That night the low was 62 degrees, and chorus frogs chattered in temporary pools. In time the white flowers decorating the blackberry canes would make dark fruit, and these seemingly benign bulls would battle to sire calves that would take tentative steps through green grass on another late April day. Somehow, it seemed, life on the prairie was in order, at least for a while. The old rhythms, abandoned for nearly a century and a half, had realigned themselves in a ceremony of buffalo and grass.

CICADA SPRING

On a cool wet day in the middle of May, my wife came home with a bag of groceries in one hand and a perplexed look on her face, muttering about insects at the door. "There's a bunch of strange-looking bugs lined up on the fence," she said. "They're bright gold, they've got red eyes, and they're just sitting there, staring."

It had been an unusual May along the banks of the Caney River in northeast Oklahoma. Unseasonably cool, extraordinarily wet. Therefore, any mention of immobile insects didn't immediately incite much interest. We'd had only three days of sunshine through the third week of May. Not exactly the kind of weather to jump-start insect engines.

Still, curiosity won out, and I ambled out into a dreary, drizzly day to see what she was talking about. And there they were, lined up on the fence, on tree limbs, under the eaves, arranged in a seemingly comatose state. Hundreds of insects and an equal number of abandoned exoskeletons stuck to tree trunks and exterior walls. It was a scene that could have been lifted from some low-budget Japanese horror movie: *Invasion of the "Magicicadas."* The arrival of Brood IV had begun.

Unfortunately for a natural phenomenon that happens only every seventeen years, the 2015 emergence of periodical cicadas, in our neck of the woods at least, corresponded with some of the worst-possible weather that an infrequent visitor could venture into. The rain was incessant, record setting. And the constant drizzly overcast kept temperatures below normal. So after burrowing up and out of the soil, the cicadas sat still and waited for better weather. And they did so in silence, strange for an insect that's programmed to wail throughout the day in long, buzzing trills orchestrated to attract romance and to do so at high volume and in great numbers.

But sit quietly was, at the moment, all these heralded visitors could do, because as cicada luck would have it, the fat little bugs with their protruding eyes had emerged into a world not quite right for reproductive frenzy. It remained overcast and cool for several more days, and *Magicicada cassini* was left with little recourse other than to add extra hours onto the seventeen years they'd spent underground, sipping fluids extracted from plant roots. And so they sat, red-orange eyes boring into damp gray space, awaiting increased warmth and sunlight. They seemed like cicada statuary: gold thoraxes and abdomens drying to brown, splitting to reveal black thoraxes and abdomens, supporting orange-tinted clear wings with black veins, orange legs locked onto whatever structure offered shelter, seemingly content to stay comatose until the return of normal May weather.

Brown exoskeleton shucks littered trees and outbuildings for days, and still the shrill keening of calling males failed to reverberate. In time, I began to wonder if an unusually wet spring would nullify a highly anticipated natural occurrence that required nearly two decades of development to transpire. Then, after several days of nervous anticipation, the sun came out, the temperature shot up, and the trees came alive with crooning cicadas.

Previously I'd never been fortunate enough to be living in the right place at the right time to experience this unique natural phenomenon. As a kid I'd mostly grown up with the great summer trilling of *Tibicen canicularis*, the ubiquitous dog-day cicada that year after year produced a near-deafening chorus during the heat of August. Later in life, during summers along the Canadian River, my Labrador retriever and I would walk the riverbank so he could hunt for cicadas that launched from sunflower stalks with a shrieking whir, allowing a hundred pounds of black Lab the opportunity to munch them like candy. But never before had periodical cicadas of the seventeen-year variety literally landed on my doorstep like these ubiquitous arrivals from the 2015 brood.

The droning, buzzing trill of our resident annual cicadas paled before the clamor of the little black bugs with the big red-orange eyes. It seemed that the individual *Magicicada* song was higher in pitch and less blasting than that of their annually appearing cousins. But the newcomers' incredible numbers more than made up for their less obtrusive caterwauling. The din soon spread through the tall hardwoods bordering the Caney River, then up the river's tributaries.

A trail bordering Pond Creek in northern Osage County soon looked like *Magicicada* Armageddon. Dead cicadas, parts of dead cicadas, and a scattering of cellophane wings littered the trail while live cicadas rasped from a canopy of Shumard oak, sycamore, pecan, and green ash. Farther west, in the Nature Conservancy's Tallgrass Prairie Preserve, the insects covered sycamores and chinquapin oaks growing along Sand Creek. Walking the trail that paralleled the stream caused an eruption of periodical cicadas from all manner of limbs and foliage, replete with buzzes of protest interrupting a love crooning that, in the aggregate, added energy to the atmosphere.

I wondered if the cicada congregation would suddenly grow silent, like a movie sound track coming to an end. But the bugs had life-or-death business to attend to and they kept at it, the chorus and the number of cicadas slowly ebbing. I saw my last live *Magicicada* on June 18. After that, there wasn't much left to do but daydream about what a cicada nymph might be doing underground for the next seventeen long years and estimate the odds of my presence on this planet when the next brood came calling.

Salt Creek begins in southern Kansas amid hills studded with pale gray limestone. Its origins are in a particularly beautiful part of the Flint Hills—a landscape rocky and wild, with oaks, willows, buttonbush, and slender sycamores defining the places where seeps and springs turn into rivulets and then into the little headwaters tributaries that coalesce into a proper stream. Salt Creek, emboldened by all this input, carves a twisting course over limestone bedrock, occasionally bouncing over fractured geology resulting in handsome, if not spectacularly tall, waterfalls.

At its headwaters, Salt Creek drains mostly grassland. Still, there are scattered woodland groves that condense into a gallery forest as the stream drops south across the Oklahoma state line and eventually widens. By the time it reaches the community of Shidler, Salt Creek has added a bit more girth due to the influx of larger tributaries. It has also added a bordering strip of forest that includes some massive bur oak and sycamore trees. Following a few snaking miles, Salt Creek flows through the ghost town of Burbank, drops south to pass through the small town of Fairfax, then curls southwest to merge with the broad Arkansas River.

During this journey, the stream flows some 60 miles and drains 840 square miles of tallgrass prairie. The average gradient is about six and a half feet per mile, with large quiet pools separated by swift riffles. Because it drains mostly grassland and cuts a valley through dense layers of limestone, the stream is generally clear, growing murky following thunderstorms. Salt Creek is a mostly mild-mannered stream but one with a quick temper. Storms in the region can dump inches of water in a short amount of time, resulting in floods that rise quickly and recede just as fast. Evidence of the violent nature of this flooding can be seen in debris lodged twenty feet or more high in the branches of streamside hardwoods.

There isn't much cropland along Salt Creek except in the wider valleys near the stream's juncture with the Arkansas. Mostly, this prairie miniriver meanders through native grassland hosting cattle and the occasional cowboy. Federally funded reservoirs have been planned for the stream, but for now Salt Creek still flows freely from start to finish.

The small towns bordering Salt Creek were generally thriving until about midway through the last century. Then oil production began to wane, and populations shrank as commerce and people drifted elsewhere. Today these once-bustling communities are borderline ghost towns. Burbank was a place where gunfights were routine when thousands flocked here early in the 1900s during one of the richest oil strikes in the Osage Nation. Today it's mostly limestone shells of empty buildings, a few aging citizens, and a reputation that once included swindlers, drug dealers, murderers, cardsharps, and prostitutes. Birds nest in these old limestone buildings, and modern traffic bypasses the rapidly decaying boomtown.

Seen from above in the summertime, Salt Creek is a slim ribbon of dark green timber bordering bright water, a silver snake undulating across rocky, jade-colored prairie. The stream is floatable in the spring and autumn rainy seasons, and from a canoe there's a distinct wilderness feel to it, a sense that arises from the remoteness, the absence of humanity, the bountiful wildlife, and the fact that the land is much the same as it was when the Osages had their camps along its banks, except for a few leftover oilfield blemishes.

From a canoe on a bright spring morning, you might see a northern harrier sweep past, toting prey in its talons, while great horned owls ponder Salt Creek comings and goings from the limbs of streamside bur oaks. Carolina wrens busily check out nesting space inside weathered tree stumps, while white-breasted nuthatches circle oaks of sturdy girth, hoping to glean nourishment from their corky, deeply furrowed bark.

April is always a good time to be on the water, especially when the waxy green of new boxelder leaves contrast with the shiny gray spring feathers of blue-gray gnatcatchers. These tiny mockingbird look-alikes seem constantly on the move through the foliage, their hissing, buzzing voices joined by the brassy calls of northern flickers and the chatter of red-headed woodpeckers, the latter prone to fuss among themselves as they search for sustenance.

At the end of one sleek pool where the stream curls tightly around a bend and drops into a choppy riffle, a cobble of limestone outwash sometimes provides a rocky refuge for an American bittern. The bird remains upright and still as a fence post, neck up and outstretched, bill pointed toward the heavens. This is a bird well suited for hiding in the open. A drab suit of pale breast feathers, adorned with darker brown streaks, allows the bittern to pass itself off as some small obscure portion of natural streamside statuary.

Early in spring, limestone outcrops bordering Salt Creek are adorned with sprays of golden yellow, the trumpetlike tubular flowers of wild currants. The showy blossoms dominate the onset of the growing season with their brightness. The region drained by Salt Creek is often plagued by fickle spring weather, and late freezes are not uncommon. But when frost danger subsides in a few weeks, these stream bottoms and adjoining grasslands will explode into a kaleidoscope of floral color.

Early in April, the display mostly consists of tough little wild mustards, many of them nonnative species. And because they flower at a time when competition for pollinators is not particularly fierce, floral cosmetics are oftentimes less than showy. All that's really needed is enough sexual equipment to get the job done. So with assistance from a few sunny days and a few early-flying insects, these ground-hugging plants, mostly annuals, are set to reproduce for yet another year.

These invasive forbs are remarkably capable of discovering a small available niche in an established environment, then settling themselves into it. It's a trait admirably inherent in generalist species that move easily from place to place and then literally put down roots at the slightest opportunity. Over the years, European immigrants have proven themselves to be especially adept at gaining an uninvited foot-hold.

On the other hand, early spring's delicately beautiful anemones, native to this place and white as snowflakes amid last year's dried grasses, have the allure of a beauty queen compared to many of the transients. They also have the toughness needed to survive late frosts. Anemones open when early bees and flies are active, close when they aren't. Most of the early flowers have a fine coating of hairs that act as a down coat when the weather cools. They've evolved to bend with spring's tempestuous weather moods, then bounce back when the weather becomes more flower friendly. A native plant's best defense against being ousted by nonnative invaders is the fact that its genetic roots have been part of the prairie's complex weather for tens of thou-sands of years. Nothing provides a better foundation for a long-term relationship than simple familiarity. Invasive plants can find those minuscule niches and spread quickly. But over the long haul the natives, if left to their own devices and not weakened by unnatural stress, have a decent chance of prevailing over many intruders.

Anemones are the floral version of lasciviousness compared to other early Salt Creek bloomers, especially the bluets and spring beau-ties that sometimes carpet the brown remains of last year's growing season. These, plus the tiny pale violets that flower when winter and spring play tug-of-war, can be a joy to behold for those weary of winter. Plus some of these early bloomers supply nutritious corms for mam-mals in need of quick carbohydrates, while their flowers, tiny as they are, loom large as a food source for equally tiny insects.

In the first half of the twentieth century, when adjoining oil fields were producing abundant petroleum, Salt Creek suffered from well site runoff—saltwater brine and untreated raw sewage flowing from boomtowns that never entertained a notion of environmental hygiene. But by the latter part of the century, oil production slowed to a trickle compared to a peak in the first half. Over time the boomtowns went bust, federal regulations halted the outflow of untreated municipal wastes, and Salt Creek became a much healthier stream.

A testimonial to improved water quality can be found in the inverte-brate life that once again prospers in Salt Creek. The presence of cer-tain aquatic insect species indicates that years of abuse didn't totally undermine the health of the stream. On some spring mornings, living proof flutters past in the form of a dark gray stonefly about two inches long. Eventually the insect settles down, seemingly content to soak up sunlight from atop an upturned and flood-ravaged johnboat. Later in the day, a peek under a rock discloses a stout mayfly nymph, a species generally found in well-oxygenated, uncontaminated water.

In the early 1950s, a pair of state wildlife department fish biologists sampling Salt Creek termed it potentially one of the most biologically productive of its type in the region. As they pointed out in a paper penned for the Oklahoma Academy of Science in 1962, "Salt Creek has been held in high regard by bass and sunfish anglers in the past, and there has also been some limited commercial fishing activity in the lower two miles of the stream in recent years. However it is periodically subjected to pollution from oil field brine wastes on the upper part of the watershed, and the effluents are often so toxic that the desirable fish population is eradicated. The elimination of this harmful practice, and that of introducing untreated sewage, would greatly enhance the opportunities of sport fishermen in the future."

Fortunately for Salt Creek, all the above came to pass. Also, the stream frequently purges itself with floods, and maybe that has been part of its salvation. Local legend has it that the stream, normally twenty to thirty feet wide, once swelled to two miles across during a notable spring flood. Most likely that was an exaggeration of at least a mile and three-quarters, but at times floodwaters have spread a quarter of a mile into the bottomland bordering the stream's mouth.

Farm fields bordering the merging of Salt Creek and the Arkansas are prone to flooding and tend to stay that way for days when water in the Arkansas remains too high to accept all of Salt Creek's frothy burden. Such floods have been the norm for thousands of years, and accepting nature's inevitabilities is the price of doing business in the fertile bottomland ... and also the reason that the bottomland remains so fertile.

By the end of April, canoeing is still mostly good on some of the southern Flint Hills streams, but only if spring rains continue to supply a floatable current. When they do, it's hard not to stop often and take pictures when large purple violets line the banks of a stream like Salt Creek, their rich hues intensified by a backdrop of pale gray limestone. Scattered throughout the stream bank are veins of spent mussel shells, many as big as a man's hand, the nacre as shiny as if machine polished. Some are a milky white, some pink, some purple.

In places where the dark earth has been peeled away by the current, pale layers of accumulated mussel shells form distinct veins in the exposed banks, almost like albino seams of coal. Sycamore trees, limbs pale as aged bone, fly new grayish green leaves as April fades into history. Spotted sandpipers perch on larger rocks in the current, pumping their nervous posteriors, fluttering more than flying downstream when alarmed.

Longer, deeper pools hold flocks of ducks—mallards, wood ducks, teal. The nervous wood ducks erupt into the air with a splash of wing tips, flying downstream only as far as the next pool. Sandpipers teeter, wood ducks keen, mallards quack in wild disharmony. Around a bend the mood is more somber—a fox squirrel and a big water snake are locked in what appears to be a battle to the death amid the exposed roots of a massive bur oak.

By midmorning, the warming water has induced an airborne mayfly ballet, the insects' wings catching the sunlight as if cut from tiny shards of glass. Shrubby buckeyes with yellow-green leaves grow below the limestone bluffs where the soil is deepest, and several banded water snakes snooze in the sun on a big limestone slab hanging out over the current.

In places where the woods open up to reveal the rolling prairie beyond, limestone outcroppings pop up through the grass like rows of small gray tombstones. The grass, green as any fabled Irish dell, provides the perfect landing strip for an upland sandpiper. The graceful migrant drops from the sky to settle upon one of the limestone outcroppings. Once at rest on this upright chunk of gray stone, the long-legged sandpiper stows each wing with a motion that's almost theatrical.

Not far away, a farmer cutting alfalfa hay captures the interest of a northern harrier. The hawk flies slow and low behind the tractor, watching for mice or rabbits frantic to escape the roaring machine. Two barred owls gaze with indifference from atop a spreading streamside sycamore, while a longnose gar weighing twenty pounds or more creases the surface of a quiet pool. The slightest splash seems to inspire rapidly twittered couplets from a male indigo bunting, a small songbird whose dark feathers glow iridescent blue in spring sunlight.

A red-headed woodpecker hammers away at a dying streamside tree while a crow-size pileated woodpecker flies overhead. The pileated's alarm call recalls the urgency of a woman's frantic screaming, the bird's bright red Woody Woodpecker topknot gleaming like a crimson banner. Nearby an ancient bur oak, a grand old tree with a circumference of ten feet or more, appears ready to abandon its role as historian of Salt Creek's centuries. Beavers have girdled the oak, and soon it will topple into the pool to serve as fish shelter, the final chapter in a life that began before the time of George Washington. Even as it dies, the massive oak will dominate the stream bank until a strong wind finishes what the beavers started. An impressive skeleton soon to be, the tree's lower limbs seem bigger than most of the trees it overshadows.

By late May, life in and along Salt Creek begins to reach a seasonal climax. Orangethroat darters, bottom-hugging minnow-size fish clinging to rocks lining spring-fed feeder streams, display bright orange and blue breeding colors. Red shiners flash crimson fins. Blanchard's cricket frogs announce mating urgency in tones sounding more like the metallic rattling of insects than the seasonal calling of amphibians.

On this humid afternoon, clouds skating on a south wind deliver the low gray promise of thunderstorms. Gray tree frogs trill that rain is inevitable. Butter yellow and brown wood duck ducklings, alarmed by a predator either real or imagined, disappear into a thick patch of aquatic herbs called water-willow. The plants, which produce rank growth in midsummer, are spotted with purplish white flowers that provide a canopy over a shallow channel and thus excellent escape cover for the baseball-size young. Tall prairie wildflowers, whipped by the wind, include white fleabane, lavender and white penstemons, snowy white larkspurs, fiery orange butterfly milkweed, and the electric pink of sensitive-briar.

The flowers draw swarms of orange and yellow butterflies. Cascading riffles crawl with tiny crayfish and bright yellow stonefly nymphs. Streamside vegetation includes the purple flowers of leadplant and leather flower. Towering pecan trees drop pale yellow flowers that gather in an eddy's backwater swirl. The spent flowers signal that the mast-producing season is under way and that in a few months squirrels, blue jays, and young anglers with bulging pockets will gather to partake of this healthy and delicious repast.

By June, Salt Creek's increasingly lavish surge of life has turned the stream into a water garden. Mats of aquatic water crowfoot clog several pools, the plant's tiny white and yellow flowers blooming both above and below the waterline. Water-willow, a *Justicia*, now dominates the riffles, its flowers perched a foot or so above the dark leafy stems rooted in the streambed.

Among the aquatic species growing in or at the edge of the stream are water buttercup, with its numerous small yellow flowers, and arrowhead plant, with its white flowers and big heart-shaped leaves. Many of these aquatics hold the shed exoskeletons of dragonflies, the tough outer skins clinging to numerous stems. Each translucent shuck indicates where a larval form climbed from the water to transform into a winged hunter blessed with the aerodynamic agility of a hummingbird. Many of these primitive insects are, upon maturity, as colorful as the brightest warblers chattering from nearby treetops.

While dragonflies dance across the air, dainty blue damselflies perch on plants growing in streamside shadows. Others occupy pale limestone, while a few grace the pink and purple nacre of mussel shells. A pair of Graham's crayfish snakes, slim and handsome in lengthwise stripes of brown and yellow, are stoically intertwined on a sycamore limb extending out over the current.

Even though the life force swells as summer advances, the comfort level drops somewhat as maddening deerflies draw blood and gnats become bothersome as they attempt to sip eye fluid. These aggravating insects mingle with small mayflies dancing over rocky riffles, the latter displaying clear wings and reddish brown abdomens, their nuptial flight arousing the appetites of a variety of flycatchers.

A green underwater stockpile beside a beaver burrow indicates where the industrious rodents have stored trimmings from both sycamore and green ash trees. Both three-toed and ornate box turtles prowl the uplands. Leopard frogs and tiny brick red toadlets, each barely an inch long and still showing a stump of a tadpole tail, congregate around small streamside pools. The final exhibit in this midsummer wildlife show is a big snapping turtle exiting a pool where slim spotted gars cruise algae-stained depths.

True summertime along Salt Creek begins in early June, and sometimes, if the spring rains continue into summer, the current remains strong enough for canoeing. Even so, summer heat is setting in, and the stream grows richly streaked with bright green filamentous algae. A young raccoon is now old enough to practice foraging techniques on its own in shallow water. Rust-colored fox squirrels chase each other across a bur oak limb extending out over a long pool, and gars splash at the surface of quiet pools turning the color of old army uniforms.

Herons appear to be stalking fish around every watery curve. A green heron launches skyward from exposed bur oak roots that shake as the current rushes through the tangle. A yellow-crowned night heron seems to disappear into the subdued light of a shadowy bend, colors blending perfectly with dappled sunlight. Prowling crows flush a pair of barred owls from a sycamore, the attackers raging and ranting their call to arms.

One of the owls flees into the shade of the adjoining oak woods. The other flies a few yards farther, then tries to land on a slim flexible limb. However, the maneuver backfires and the owl loses its footing, but does manage to spear another limb with its talons before tumbling into the water. For several seconds the bird hangs above the water like an upside-down monkey, then struggles to right itself with an explosive burst of wing power. The commotion inspires five whitetail does plus a yearling fawn to race from under the oaks and splash across the stream, seeking more peaceful premises to resume their noonday nap.

Salt Creek's pools remain clear, but the water is rapidly turning dark olive green as increasing sunlight spurs microscopic algae growth. It's still clear enough to see the pale circular patterns of sunfish nests, with any accumulating silt being quickly swept away by attending males. Yet without a doubt Salt Creek is slipping into the long, heavy, superheated days of midsummer. Proof can be found in the swarming insects frequenting the increasingly tepid pools, as well as in the abundance of young and eager appetites converging to eat them.

Summer along Salt Creek is a drowsy, hazy festival of extreme heat, rapidly warming water, and life in the shade. Pools shrink, riffles trickle, and in places herbage like water-willow colonizes long stretches of the stream, providing a wet jungle for ducklings to hide in. The aquatic herbs also provide a natural high-rise structure for a variety of aquatic insects and spiders. July and August heat tends to flip a switch, at which point most activity becomes nocturnal. Life continues and even increases, with myriad creatures learning how to eat and not be eaten. In summer's deep heat, the voices of Salt Creek are night sounds—the electric buzz of cicadas, the clicking of cricket frogs sounding like pebbles colliding, the basso of bullfrogs, the snarling of raccoons fighting over a scrap of food, the eerie screams of owls, the misery in the squeals of a rabbit that will soon sate the appetite of a coyote.

Eventually autumn rains will break the heat, tree roots will cease to tug at the water table, receding daylight will reduce the amount of microscopic plant life suspended in the water, and the olive green cast will clear. During quiet winter months, the prairie stream will experience a transformation as it prepares for the fierce green energy of another spring. Waterfalls will again bounce over limestone ledges, and bald eagles will watch from sycamore boughs as fish move from pool to pool. Fortunately, winters aren't long here at the southern end of the Flint Hills, and soon warming temperatures will announce the imminent return of another April.

Brown-headed cowbirds aren't pretty like the gaudy male songbirds of our woodlands. Their traditional habitat was, literally, where the buffalo roamed, and that's a place where being eye-catching can be synonymous with a death warrant.

Instead, like grassland sparrows, prairie grouse, and others of their ilk that prefer to remain alive long enough to reproduce, cowbirds evolved to fit in. The female is nondescript brown, the male more dapper in black topped by a brown head. Both are amply lovely if you appreciate nature's way of placing environmental function ahead of vanity. Eye-catching adornment might draw some admiring glances if you're a fashionable young woman at a shopping mall, but in the wild it'll get a bird killed in a world of tan grass, gray rock, and brown buffalo dung.

Brown-headed cowbirds, members of the successful blackbird tribe, long ago evolved away from the flashy looks more suited to the dark green shadows of the forest and instead adopted a lifestyle in sync with open country—particularly grassland that supported buffalo herds. Bison of the American steppes were an insect magnet and therefore a cowbird magnet as well. Flies attracted to the herds and bugs dislodged by grazing were a movable feast. Brown-headed cowbirds zealously followed their pantry on the hoof, and in doing so they became the vagabonds of the North American hinterland.

It was a successful adaptation until Europeans arrived with their guns, cows, and plows. The newcomers cleared the land and stocked the newly created pastures with cattle. At the same time, some of their more resilient kin headed west to kill the buffalo. For cowbirds, the demise of the buffalo meant evolutionary crisis. But true to tribal genetics, they adapted quickly when domestic livestock became the new buffalo in the cowbird world.

Cowbirds expanded their range to wherever a bovine hoisted its tail next to a fence. Yet in doing so the species created enemies. The cowbird had long ago forsaken the traditional stay-at-home lifestyle of "good" birds. Instead, upon mating, brown-headed cowbirds searched for an existing nest constructed by a different species, left an egg in it, and moved on with the restless herds.

Sometimes the parasitized nest builders would recognize an alien egg among its own, sometimes it wouldn't. If the cowbird egg hatched, the adoptive parents would be faced with feeding a chick that was often larger, more aggressive, and ultimately more successful than the other nestlings. If all went well, the cowbird chick was the benefactor of a reproductive strategy that was good for the adult cowbirds, good for an impostor nestling with a large appetite, but a strain on foster parents and any noncowbird baby birds that ended up with the short end of the worm. Over time, many grassland species learned to give the alien cowbird egg a toss or even build another nest layer atop it. But when cowbirds began to move into cow pastures back east, their procreation tactics affected a number of naive songbirds and drew society's ire. Unfortunately for the vagabonds of the plains, people had an anthropomorphic tendency to despise them for a survival strategy that, for thousands of years, had simply come naturally.

This was totally unfair, of course. Brown-headed cowbirds aren't people. They don't perch on a branch plotting ways to forsake their child-rearing duties. They don't snicker at the thought that their proclivity for brood parasitism might push species uneducated in the ways of cowbirdism to the edge of extinction. What they do started with the buffalo, and if we're going to be anthropomorphic, there's a certain romance surrounding a bird that adapted to wind, grass, and animals with restless feet, millions and millions of them. Bison and cowbirds were roamers all and allies forever, it would have seemed. Yet the buffalo never were a match for a steel plow and a .45-70 bullet, and cowbirds couldn't contend with the human propensity to judge wildlife under the auspices of so-called civilized values.

Personally, I've always been a fan of the brown-headed cowbird. Yet few others seem to share my view, not even dedicated birders with their legendary zeal for anything with feathers. I believe the male cowbird's purling song has the sound of splashing water in it, and his mating persistence does have some anthropomorphic qualities, namely, the dogged determination of high schoolers exploring their own awakening biology. Also, throughout my life I've watched cowbirds live their lives around cattle, and they've come to represent an integral part of the grassland-grazer environment. Which is why, now that bison are back on the tallgrass in representative numbers, watching a cowbird land on a shaggy brown back has certain time travel implications.

A trip to the Nature Conservancy's Tallgrass Prairie Preserve in late April begins with the anticipation of seeing buffalo calves, the newborns' orange coats standing out against a backdrop of bright green grass. As you watch the calves buck and butt heads with the sheer ecstasy of being alive in a vast and bountiful world, brown-headed cowbirds are there with them, their invigorated voices signaling that the mating season has arrived, that it's time to renew the species without the drudgery of building nests and feeding fledglings. It's a cowbird's heritage, after all, for as long as the wind blows free and bison once again inhabit open spaces.

As for anyone adamant about imposing personal morals on a bird doing nothing more than what nature prepared it to do, there is now scientific research that offers this much-maligned creature a reprieve that's long overdue. In a story printed in the George Miksch Sutton Avian Research Center's online magazine in 1999, biologist Don Wolfe reports that cowbird nest parasitism isn't as injurious as once thought.

According to Wolfe, research on brown-headed cowbird nest parasitism has shown that the impact has been largely overestimated. He points out that if a host species population was severely affected by cowbirds, then the cowbirds' reproductive strategy couldn't have worked over the long term—there'd be no suitable hosts left to raise cowbird young.

The Sutton Center's own research in Oklahoma documented that species with the highest rates of brood parasitism had nesting success rates for parasitized nests equal to or higher than unparasitized nests.

Wolfe said they discovered that orchard orioles, parasitized 38 percent of the time, had 67 percent brood-rearing success rates for parasitized nests yet only 32 percent success in raising eggs to fledglings in unparasitized nests.

Wolfe reported that while red-winged blackbird nests were parasitized some 22 percent of the time, these same nests managed a success rate of 28 percent. Unparasitized redwing nests achieved a success rate of 29 percent. Dickcissel nests were parasitized by cowbirds approximately 19 percent of the time yet managed a brood-rearing success rate of 30 percent, while unparasitized nests achieved 33 percent success.

Sutton Center researchers found that species most adversely affected by cowbird parasitism generally are parasitized less frequently. Grasshopper sparrows with cowbird eggs deposited in their nests were found to achieve brood success only 5 percent of the time, compared to 33 percent for unparasitized nests. Yet the studies indicated that grasshopper sparrow nests received cowbird eggs only 7 percent of the time. Eastern meadowlarks receiving cowbird eggs managed a 13 percent success rate, while unparasitized nests climbed to 24 percent. However, eastern meadowlark nests were targeted by cowbirds at a rate of only 6 percent.

Wolfe concluded that brown-headed cowbirds have evolved a successful reproductive strategy that's much more in sync with their surroundings than previously considered. He suggested that researchers continue to take an open-minded look at the intricacies of cowbird-egg host relationships, because there is still much to learn.

Learning the facts seems much more fair than blanket condemnation based on human morality rather than natural science. Brown-headed cowbirds have long shared a space in grassland ecological patterns, patterns we are just now beginning to understand in our haste to document that which is rapidly disappearing. I can only hope that the scientific community will continue to delve into the reproductive ways of this much-blasphemed prairie dweller. And maybe someday those in charge of such matters will change its common name to buffalo bird, one that acknowledges the old way of life and a strategy for survival that arose out of necessity, like it or not.

Thoughts of late June in the Flint Hills call to mind the gentle arc of prairie coneflowers with their drooping red and yellow petals. By the time these flowers fade, the prairie will have slipped into the golden season of deep summer, a time when sunflowers predominate and grasses take on the subtle shades of approaching maturity.

The time of the summer solstice, the longest day of the year, is no longer celebrated as it was by forgotten people we now dismiss as uncivilized. Instead, the season's comings and goings are taken for granted by societies wedded to technology, people who find their seasonal comfort level through the convenience of air conditioners and furnaces burning fossil fuels. Still, here in the tallgrass country, the pace of daily activity seems celebration enough as every living thing, from birds to reptiles to cowboys cutting hay, looks upon the solstice as a period of great energy and fecundity.

Not far from the headwaters of Hominy Creek, the whistling calls of upland sandpipers circling overhead mingle with the worried chatter of mother sandpipers on the ground. Each agitated female strives to keep her young safe, at a time when it seems so many predators are obligated to eat them. To the casual observer, it might appear that spring's crop of spindly-legged butterscotch and brown upland sandpiper chicks would be depleted in a matter of hours. They seem so vulnerable.

Yet the young birds are surprisingly quick to flee, seek shelter, and blend into background vegetation. Even so, mother sandpipers continue to fret both on the wing and while pacing the prairie. After all, they've migrated from South America to rear their young in these grasslands, and for upland sandpipers, rearing young is the task they were designed to accomplish.

The thick heat and humidity of the season do little to deter the incessant territorial chatter of male indigo buntings, sparrow-size birds that shine like polished blue chrome when the sun strikes them. The nondescript brown females are easily overlooked, but the little males make up for their diminutive size by perching proudly on a tree branch, tossing their heads back, gaping wide, and belting the broad sky with a repertoire comprised mostly of couplets. These rapidly repeated phrases tend to blend into a pleasing warble, broadcast to any competitor within hearing by a shining prairie jewel decked out in iridescent feathers.

Mixed among the lush June grasses, now several feet tall, are the purples and pinks of prairie clover and sabatia, one of the prairie's most visually stunning flowers. Sabatia, a member of the gentian family, displays a simple yet beautiful inflorescence that's a true hot pink. It's also radiantly at its peak around the time of the solstice. The glaring, sensual color contrasts with the bluish green of rapidly maturing Indiangrass and bluestems.

Harder to see but certainly worth searching for are the pale lavender trumpet-shaped blossoms of ruellia. This beautiful flower comes along when the prairie grasses are getting taller, generally about knee high if not overgrazed. Sometimes you almost have to part the bluestem tussocks with your hands to find the tallgrass prairie's wild petunia. But once discovered, this member of the acanthus family proves to be not only photogenic but also worthy of the many cultivars commonly grown for landscape plantings.

Normally a southern Flint Hills June is a rainy month, allowing for lots of humidity and daytime highs that average in the low to mid-nineties around the solstice. Warm, humid days blessed with ample rainfall enrich the growing season, providing a lushness that's responsible for the region's reputation for fattening cattle at an accelerated rate.

By late June, wild turkey hens are off the nest and gleaning insects, usually with an observant procession of poults in tow. Young turkeys learn much about the world and their successful role in it by watching their mother. She's a bird that does an admirable job, albeit a nervous one, of feeding while at the same time watching out for the many predators that would relish a turkey dinner, even a lightweight one.

Today a hen and her young are searching for grasshoppers in the tall grass bordering Hominy Creek. Prairie streams can be exceptionally pretty in June, and some like Hominy Creek rise as mere trickles amid the flowers of open grassland, then quickly set to work carving streambeds that flow over nearly solid stone. Eventually they connect dozens of deeper pools carved out of limestone and sandstone bedrock, perfect swimming holes for ranch kids, a panting dog or two, and an assortment of frogs, turtles, and snakes.

As Hominy Creek begins to dig a deeper canyon, it adds a border of scattered trees and shrubs. A number of worn trails leading to and from the water are obviously beaver work. Along the trails, you'll find the stumps of freshly cut shrubs, plus the sign of branches that have been dragged into the deeper pools. Late June beaver fodder may range from herbaceous plants like giant ragweed, with its soft stems, to tougher woody shrubs like rusty blackhaw, with its waxy green leaves that tend to linger on the stems even when stashed underwater.

Beavers share these stone-bottomed basins that serve as their commissaries with diamondback water snakes, nonpoisonous yet sullen of temperament and growing as big around as a large man's forearm. Both beavers and snakes are serenaded throughout the summer by Blanchard's cricket frogs, olive brown amphibians about the size of the first joint of an adult thumb. Male cricket frogs advertise for females with a mechanical clicking sound, and both males and females are fond of taking wild leaps into the water when disturbed, only to wheel back around once underwater. In a matter of seconds, they've paddled back to the place they first fled.

By mid-June, the beaver pools will be encircled by a lush growth of prairie forbs and grasses. One of the most lovely is monarda, a knee-high mint with large tropical-looking flowers ascending a tall stalk, their perfume lemony but not sweet, a spicy outdoor smell that seems to intoxicate butterflies. Green sunfish gather near the surface of each pool below the purple reflections of these flowers, searching for grasshoppers that misjudged their leaps. Soft brown droppings along the stream bank announce that white-tailed deer, maybe a doe and her fawns, came to drink sometime after midnight.

A spiny softshell turtle, an odd-looking animal with a slim piggish snout and a leathery carapace, may surface to study its surroundings. Softshells can accelerate quickly underwater, and the reason why is evident when the turtle uses her flippers to steady herself at the edge of the bank. The size of the webbed feet is astounding, and the turtle, with her long rubbery nose and huge appendages, looks almost comical. However, to the prey she successfully captures and consumes, this softshell must resemble some terrible monster haunting their worst nightmares.

Clouds begin to thicken in the afternoon, and cloud-shrouded days along Hominy Creek tend to draw trills from gray tree frogs. The bark-colored amphibians are difficult to spot as they cling to the tree trunks. When storms are approaching, these small amphibians with their suction-cup toe disks prove to be the streamside equivalent of TV weather news. And while the tree frogs talk of rain, the stream chimes in with the cascading sound of waterfalls and riffles. The current carries an olive tint from the summer algae bloom, and an ample amount of water still tumbles over bedrock waterfalls, falls that sometimes drop seven feet or more before splashing into awaiting pools.

On this particular afternoon a green heron, perched on a sycamore branch near a waterfall, seems reluctant to take flight, a sign that the fishing has been good here on the afternoon of the solstice. The waterfall belies the stereotype of dry native grassland as it tosses spray several feet into the air, providing a fine mist for a variety of wildflowers growing along the rocky bank.

Dense clusters of eastern gamagrass, a tall coarse plant with large seeds and leaves, dominate the bank in several places. Back in the shade of the oak groves, the call of a yellow-billed cuckoo reverberates like a sound track from an old Tarzan movie. In pioneer days, this bird was known as a rain crow and allegedly forecast thunderstorms with its raucous calling. The cuckoo loves to feed on caterpillars, insect larvae with huge appetites for the leaves of streamside plants.

Starry campion, a lovely shade-tolerant white flower on a stem some two feet tall, blooms in the woodland shadows. The campions, with their four white deeply notched ray flowers, look more like something you'd find growing in the Smoky Mountains. Nearby, the trunks from a small grove of hickory trees are spread out on the ground, leveled by beavers. Just before dark, a yearling whitetail buck, pronged antlers wrapped in a nourishing protective tissue called velvet, steps from the shadows to sip from a pool fed by a low waterfall.

The following morning, the strong thunderstorm that dumped several inches of rain throughout the watershed begins to wind down by nine o'clock, leaving the humidity at nearly 100 percent in a sauna of bright sunlight. A common milkweed plant, flowering pink in big flashy sprays, serves as a singing perch for a wetland-loving warbler known as a common yellowthroat. The bird, with its bright yellow breast and black mask, sings a three-syllable song that's been translated as "witchery witchery witchery."

The hillsides along the stream are turning a soft pale blue, a sign that the native grasses are maturing and the reason for the common names of two of the most common species. Flowering just above the tops of the grasses are clumps of butterfly milkweed with flower clusters of bright orange, the plant letting the prairie's many butterflies know that a feast awaits if they'd just help move some pollen from one bush to another.

The natural color schemes of the solstice include the gray-green foliage of leadplant and its purple-spiked flower clusters. Dark blue prairie spiderworts continue to flower at the edge of woodlands, and the big bell-like flowers of cobaea penstemon, white with purplish streaking, seem more exotic than any introduced bloom in some downtown flower show.

In places where fingers of oak woodland creep away from the stream and out into the prairie, the dark green leaves of the trees contrast with yellow black-eyed Susans and tall prairie parsley. Dickcissels, looking like miniature meadowlarks with their bright yellow breasts, seem to sing from every shrub taller than the rapidly growing grass. Northern bobwhite quail identify themselves with sharply whistled three-note calls that say, to the human ear at least, "fer bob white." Each far-carrying outburst sends a message to the ladies that all territory claimed by both bobwhite and dickcissel song continues to be prime for nesting.

A whitetail fawn, curled up in the grass, remains motionless as its mother eases down to the stream to feed. The reddish coat and white spots blend perfectly with the natural background. It also helps that the recently born little deer, all legs and ears, remains absolutely still while the doe forages. Certainly the fawn would be prime food for predators, but an instinct to remain motionless and a lack of scent at this early age provide ample defenses that keep venison eaters dining elsewhere.

Near the clumps of grass where the fawn lies hidden, oak-shaped leaves of compass plants grace a number of tall stalks, each with flower buds about to open into showy bright yellow blooms. The compass plant, the signature midsummer flower of the prairie, derives its name from the extra-large leaves that orient their edges north and south, allowing the plant to manage its solar energy intake. Prairie plants react to their environment in many ways. Some, like compass plants, realign their solar receptors. Some open or close their stomata, tiny pores in the leaves, to manage the amount of water vapor lost during the process of photosynthesis. Some curl their leaves under the duress of the blistering heat and aridity of a prairie summer. Many have a high silicon content to deter grazers. Life's a battle to survive, especially if you're a plant that can't pull up roots and move to where the rain is falling or the temperature is more benign. Therefore, the plants of the tallgrass region have evolved means of dealing with the extremes of their environment and are truly, through thousands of years of experimentation, native to this place.

The compass plants here are tall, nearly six feet, because they've been protected from grazers by a fence along a county road. An afternoon breeze causes each to bend, as if they're bowing to the pickup truck rattling along the road and raising dust. It's a rusted old Chevy, carrying an elderly man and woman headed out to the old home place to pick blackberries, the dark purplish fruit now tart and sweet, the flavor evoking the essence of the land that nourishes it.

A painted bunting flies overhead. It's a male, and it looks like an Easter egg dipped in shades of green, raspberry, blue, red, and yellow. No other bird that frequents the tallgrass country's oak groves is so colorful, and yet when the gaudy male lands among the foliage of a post oak, he seems to disappear. Obviously this extravagant color scheme has evolved into excellent, time-tested camouflage.

Not far from the compass plants a hummingbird moth, fluttering on wings almost too fast to photograph, visits a pale lavender ruellia tucked into the shadow of a clump of little bluestem. A pair of pale brown grasshopper sparrows flutter a few feet from a similar bunch of bluestem before diving into more grass just a few feet away. At times the birds seem almost mouselike in their efforts to retreat from danger in the form of a camera-laden interloper.

Just at dusk, a thunderhead begins to mushroom tens of thousands of feet heavenward, a colossal tower of linen white bordered by bruised blue. The cloud pillar, with its potential for lightning, rain, hail, and maybe even winds that could uproot trees, frames an upland sandpiper landing on an aged wooden fence post. The bird folds its boomerang wings slowly and surveys its summer domain with what has to be some form of upland sandpiper satisfaction. The season of the solstice is winding down, the summer peaking in its lushness. Sandpiper chicks are growing fat, and more rain is on the way to nourish the creatures great and small waiting to dine on grassland bounty.

It's difficult to grow up in America's grasslands without becoming acquainted with tumblebugs. Maybe that's because a tumblebug's lifework revolves around feces, a subject that country kids are inordinately fascinated with. Plus, the visual saga of a tumblebug attempting to roll a ball of dung up an incline has Aesopian qualities that make grasshopper and ant fables pale before this seemingly herculean effort. Tumblebugs rarely succeed the first time, but they seldom tarry before reengaging the object of their frustration and giving it, once again, the old tumblebug heave-ho. This drama of pushing excrement up a hill can go on for hours and was, before television and video games, a midsummer matinee for curiosities rather easily captivated.

The tumblebug, in case you haven't met one yet, is a stoutly built blackish beetle that lives by following its nose to prime poop. Actually, the insect's olfactory receptors are located on its antennae, perfectly positioned to home in on any fresh neighborhood feces. And fresh they must be. Tumblebugs—or scarab beetles to those who can't condone country colloquialisms—can be picky when it comes to selecting the proper pat of poo for nourishment and procreation.

Scarabs are among the more interesting of the beetle tribe, varying in size, beauty, and occupation. Some scarabs dine on flower pollen, some are shiny and colorful, some excited the imaginations of ancient Egyptians. The tumblebug of America's grasslands is none of these. This beetle eats dung. It is neither colorful nor shiny. It's just a workaday insect that labors in the fields, successful as long as cattle stay regular.

The tumblebug of the prairies is a beetle of the *Canthon* species. Pairs are monogamous to some extent. Male and female work together to prepare a suitable nursery for little tumblebugs to be, the male excavating a hole in the dirt, the female attending to nesting duties.

But all must begin with a bowel movement. American grasslands were once covered with buffalo, which were then replaced by cattle, both prime tumblebug benefactors. Tumblebug dung must be fresh, so large numbers of hoofed grazers ruminate to the tumblebugs' advantage. Even so, the baking heat of a prairie summer can be desiccating. Therefore, the beetles have a slim window of opportunity for finding cow plop of proper vintage.

Fortunately, tumblebugs are hard workers. The ten- to nineteen-millimeter-long oval insects have strong, flattened, sharp-edged heads, excellent for digging. The front tibiae also are flattened, with serrations on the outer edges for cutting and shaping. Middle and hind tibiae are slender and curved for dung ball rolling and steering.

A day of dung mining begins with some scouting on the wing. Tumblebug antennae come into play as the insect seeks to detect the oftentimes not-so-sweet smell of a fresh cow patty. If all goes well, the airborne beetle locks in on a scent plume, follows the smell to its source, then drops down for a closer inspection.

If the poop pat proves to be grade A choice, the tumblebug starts to assemble dung ball raw material. This involves slicing and shaping the fresh plop so that the results can be moved to the insect's favored picnic area. The sculpting process involves head, forelegs, and maybe a few tumblebug pirouettes in a circular pattern. After just the right amount is carved away, the beetle climbs aboard and begins assembling a sphere with those tool-like forelegs.

Rounding out the dung ball involves a lot of patting, trimming, and sometimes even plastering on a "handful" here and there to achieve better symmetry. The ball is rotated a few revolutions to ensure that it meets exacting tumblebug standards. Next, the half-inch ball must be pushed to a place where the tumblebug hopes to cache its treasure and dine in peace. The beetle uses its hind legs to push, steering and steadying with fore and middle legs. This trial-and-error process is the part that has fascinated country folk for generations.

Watching a tumblebug struggle can be gritty, down-to-earth entertainment. At the same time, it's often vaudeville par excellence. The beetle routinely slips, tumbles (thus the colloquial name), or loses control of the dung ball completely. At that point, the tumblebug's trophy always rolls back downhill, because dung balls don't come equipped with brakes or consciences.

When this recalcitrant tumblebug treasure reaches the proper location, the beetle parks it and begins digging dirt from beneath the ball. Following a shallow burial, the tumblebug begins to gorge. In about a day's time, all that's left in the hole may be little more than a few coarse fibers from the dung ball and some satisfied beetle poop, signifying that the digestive process has run its course several times over.

The brood ball—the dung intended to serve as food for tumblebug larvae—is the epitome of dung ball dexterity. It's up to the male to make this objet d'art, his dung ball of dung balls, while at the same time defending it from lurking males with larceny in their tumblebug hearts. These are desperate fellows who would like nothing more than to nab a well-made sphere and use it to impress the ladies.

Male tumblebugs appear to take extra time and greater care in carving, shaping, and patting down the brood ball, striving, it seems, for perfection. Rival males frequenting the same pile of raw poop that find themselves in the presence of such a freshly made masterpiece are unabashedly eager to make it their own via a tumblebug grab and run.

Therefore, the master sculptor may be forced to fight for his brood ball during the shaping process. He may even chase away some of the females drawn to the sleekly patted ball for less larcenous purposes. However, a lady tumblebug tends to be persistent. Following a few fractious encounters, the male generally acquiesces and his newly acquired mate climbs aboard the mister's masterpiece, an anointed queen preening on her dung ball balcony.

A brood ball, following cross-country transportation (the male pushes, the female rides), ends up buried deeper than a simple food ball. Mating occurs there in the love cave, eggs are laid (an average of three or four eggs per brood), and hatched larvae develop by feeding on the dung, reaching adulthood in a month to a month and a half.

It's not an easy life, being a tumblebug, what with so much poop to roll, highway robbery commonplace, and females more inclined to

The Curious Life of the Tumblebug

hitch a ride than to get off and help push. But the beetles persevere, and the rest of the biological world benefits.

A dung beetle study conducted by the Noble Foundation on a southern Oklahoma ranch found that these beetles help control horn flies and intestinal parasites, livestock pests that cost ranchers millions of dollars. Both need fresh dung to reproduce. Scarab beetles tend to bury these harmful larvae in their dung balls, short-circuiting the troublesome parasites' life cycle. Tumblebugs in the study area buried approximately one ton of wet manure per day, increasing the land's water infiltration rate by 129 percent. Dung beetles returned to the rancher's place when he stopped spraying insecticides. The return of the tumblebug reduced overall expenditures while boosting moisture retention in an area prone to drought.

At the same time, all that manure added carbon and nutrients to the soil and helped feed essential soil microflora. Dung left to dry on the surface loses 80 percent of its nitrogen back into the atmosphere. Therefore the lowly tumblebug, nature's little engine that could, tends to be among the prairie's best recyclers, a six-legged fable-in-waiting even Aesop would have admired, had he not been so preoccupied with lowly ants and grasshoppers.

Aldo Leopold, whose book *A Sand County Almanac* helped ignite a wild-fire of American ecological consciousness in the 1970s, liked to nose around old cemeteries and ruminate about the rare plants he'd discover there. Leopold, born an Iowan, understood that a little of the old tallgrass prairie survived in those cemeteries, while beyond their boundaries most of the tillable countryside had been plowed and planted to corn.

In one essay, the sainted professor waxed poetically about *Silphium laciniatum*, the regal compass plant. Compass plant, often five feet tall or more and festooned with bright yellow flowers similar to sunflowers, begins to grace the prairie landscape at a time when the spring wildflowers begin to fade and the summer season, with its even taller wildflowers, many of them yellow, begins.

"Every July I watch eagerly a certain country graveyard that I pass in driving to and from my farm," Leopold wrote in *A Sand County Almanac.* "It is time for a prairie birthday, and in one corner of this graveyard lives a surviving celebrant of that once important event. It is an ordinary graveyard, bordered by the usual spruces, and studded with the usual pink granite or white marble headstones, each with the usual Sunday bouquet of red or pink geraniums. It is extraordinary only in being triangular instead of square, and in harboring, within the sharp angle of its fence, a pin-point remnant of the native prairie on which the graveyard was established in the 1840's. Heretofore unreachable by scythe or mower, this yard-square relic of original Wisconsin gives birth, each July, to a man-high stalk of compass plant or cutleaf Silphium, spangled with saucer-sized yellow blooms resembling sunflowers. It is the sole remnant of this plant along this highway, and perhaps the sole remnant in the western half of our county. What a thousand acres of Silphiums looked like when they tickled the bellies of the buffalo is a question never again to be answered, and perhaps not even asked."

When I reread this passage from time to time, especially in late June, I wish Leopold was still among us so that I could show him *Silphiums* tickling the bellies of buffalo at the Nature Conservancy's Tallgrass Prairie Preserve. During the week preceding the Fourth of July, a healthy patch of compass plants began to flower where several dozen young bulls like to snooze and graze. There's little doubt that even as the stout flower stalks burst into golden bloom, nearly a ton of bull bison, sleek as a show pig from all the nourishing spring grass, had his belly tickled by this statuesque plant with its big oak-shaped leaves that orient north and south.

And if I had a chance, I'd show Mr. Leopold prairie hay meadows in the region where other once-common plants spread their leaves to the sun. These plants, like Leopold's poetically immortalized *Silphiums*, still occur and retain their health because these hay meadows are mowed but haven't been grazed in decades. Here on the rocky southern prairies it was the cow, and not the plow, that banished compass plants and other "ice cream plants" from the surrounding pastures. Cattle grazed these highly nutritious and obviously tasty plants so hard that they rarely had an opportunity to restore nutrients to their roots and, ultimately, were replaced by invasive plants or others much less palatable.

So like Leopold's carefully watched Wisconsin graveyard, the old-time hay meadows tend to be living prairie museums. Walk through one in the growing season, and you'll find grasses and forbs rarely seen these days in the grazing land across the fence. Toward the middle of summer they'll be mowed down, allowed to dry in the sun, and baled for hay. But after that these meadows will recover, add leaf mass, replenish roots, and awaken the following spring, as they have since long before the first bovine came ambling up from Texas.

One of my favorite hay meadows borders Highway 60 west of Pawhuska. It belongs to a ranch whose founder came to the area as an Indian trader when the Osages established their final reservation here in the 1870s. The family has produced beef off these prairie grasslands ever since, and I have little doubt that this big hay meadow has been providing baled fodder for their horses and cattle for nearly a century and a half.

Drive by this hay meadow in mid-June, and immediately you'll notice the bright yellow *Silphium* flowers along with a lush grass with long leaves spraying up and out like water from a fountain. The grass will already have tall flower stalks fringed with reddish flowers, some of the stalks as tall as a very tall man.

The grass is *Tripsacum dactyloides*, native eastern gamagrass, the "queen of the grasses" as *Beef Magazine* described it back in 1998. According to the article, eastern gamagrass is the queen because it grows in all types of soil, tolerates drought, and produces forage with a protein content around 17 percent and a TDN (total digestible nutrients) ranking of 65 percent and, depending on soil fertility and precipitation, hay in volumes ranging from two to ten tons per acre.

Eastern gamagrass is deep rooted, able to mine water at depths that machine-sown exotic grasses can't match. It matures a little earlier than other native warm-season grasses, providing excellent grazing right after the cool-season grasses begin to go dormant and just before the peak growth of Indiangrass, switchgrass, and the bluestems. The leaves of gamagrass can store twice as much nitrogen as its sister grasses. And the plant's ability to store carbon is also prodigious, a queenly capability considering the sequestration needs presented by carbon-induced climate change.

Eastern gamagrass is a cousin to corn, and botanists have toyed with modifying the plant into a perennial food crop, alleviating the need for seasonal plowing and the ongoing soil deterioration that results. One might think that as tallgrass prairie royalty, eastern gamagrass requires rich soils and annual rainfall approaching thirty-six inches a year. Yet I've seen the plant growing quite well in the hotbed sands bordering the Canadian River in central Oklahoma, in association with sand bluestem and well west of the traditional tallgrass prairie zone.

Eastern gamagrass seems to be a plant for many districts and seasons, managing quite well in soils ranging from blackland prairies to midgrass plains or wherever the average rainfall total is high enough to support its bountiful growing habits. So why has this supergrass, a plant that evolved with the buffalo herds, been mostly off the botanical radar until the last couple of decades? Blame it on the cow and on well-developed bovine taste buds. Without a doubt, bison relished gamagrass as much as the next ungulate. But prior to fences, buffalo ate and ran—well, more of a fast walk or a modified trot, but they did keep on the move, allowing time for the plants they grazed to regain leaf mass and store nutrients in their roots, providing for healthy reemergence the following spring.

Cattle, on the other hand, have been contained in fenced pastures since the end of the open range days in the late 1800s. They return again and again to the nutritious plants they prefer, grazing them low to the ground, rarely allowing them an opportunity to recover leafy surface area. In time the favorites are weakened and replaced by less palatable plants or invasive species that cattle won't touch even though they're near starvation.

In heavily grazed pastures, eastern gamagrass was among the first to go. It hasn't remained a noticeable component of the modern prairie ecosystem simply because it didn't last long enough to get noticed. *Beef Magazine* claimed that the grass was "rediscovered" by a Missouri farmer in the 1980s.

While eastern gamagrass tends to be out of sight as well as out of mind on rangeland that's borne a heavy cow burden, I've consistently found clumps growing in hard-to-reach places along prairie streams, even in heavily grazed cattle country. At the same time, the grass has remained well represented in prairie hay meadows, in state parks and wildlife refuges, on Corps of Engineers land bordering reservoirs, and in old cemeteries throughout the tallgrass country.

Recently I found the arching leaves of gamagrass growing near a spring on the old home place, and the discovery spurred thoughts concerning the ecological resiliency of what remains of the tallgrass prairie landscape. At times it seems as if there is an unseen safe-deposit box tucked away in the prairie underground. The key to bringing the contents back to the surface includes rest if needed, fire, careful management of grazing animals, and adequate seasonal rainfall.

It's an easy combination to remember, and a conscientious steward of the land can supply all of the above except rain. Follow directions and previously unseen plants will reappear and prosper—plants that haven't been seen in decades or maybe within a lifetime. The elasticity and powers of rejuvenation in a landscape can be astounding. Yet as Aldo Leopold cautioned, the land becomes healthy and whole again only if we're wise enough to save all its parts.

When the cicadas begin to wail their loudest and the sullen midsummer heat lingers well past midnight, American lotus flowers begin to peak in the shallow water of ponds scattered across the prairie. Today lotus is found mostly in structures that collect the runoff of seeps and springs so that cattle can drink throughout the year. But back when Osage women harvested the tubers of these eye-catching plants, the blooms covered the little oxbow lakes formed when rivers like the Verdigris or Caney changed course and the old channels became catchment basins. In time they formed marshes replete with the rounded, elevated leaves of the lotus plant, stout stems crowned with a pale yellow flower as big as a man's palm and as beautiful as a fine etching.

Along Pond Creek, a stream in the southern Flint Hills, you can find mini-lakes covered with waterfowl in winter. Later, when the late July heat and haze settle in, these shallow ponds become clogged with the airborne "lily pads" of lotus. True lily pads actually rest upon the water's surface, while lotus leaves, rounded and a foot or more across, sit atop elevated stems. These large airborne leaves, accented by saucer-shaped flowers tinted to pale yellow perfection, add a touch of the exotic to any marshy basin. A lotus pond seems like Asian art come to life, and if dragonflies could recite the poetry they cleave with their wings, these little marshes would have their own haiku. Now and then a bullfrog may break in with booming percussion, but mostly it's the drone of hormonally supercharged insects that praises the monotony of midsummer humidity and the lingering heat of lotus season.

On a morning in late July, a lotus-covered marsh near Pond Creek comes alive with flying insects. At the moment, they seem drawn more to the sweet promise of flowering buttonbush than to the beauty of pale yellow lotus blooms. The white buttonbush flowers, each the size and shape of a golf ball, appeal strongly to butterflies, including the big showy species that are beginning to materialize as the season of green haze settles in.

The best time to visit a lotus pond in late July is, due to the heat, as soon as there's enough light to find your way through the vegetation. On this particular morning, record rains in May and June have propelled the grasses to waist-high heights. Unfortunately, ungrazed tallgrass can hide blackberry canes and the tiny hooked barbs of sensitive-briar within their dense blue-greenness. Even a short walk to the pond results in bare legs scratched and bleeding, but wading among the lotus blossoms relieves the discomfort with the cool ointment of dark brown marsh mud.

Red-winged blackbirds clinging to lotus stems are wary of a creature that seems to draw comfort from such a common balm as marsh mud. But blackbird disapproval does little to deter a daydreamer, especially one lost in long-ago thoughts of Osage women young and old, all laughing and gossiping as they feel for lotus tubers with practiced toes.

The Indians of the Midwest, the Osages, Omaha, Poncas, Kaws, Pawnee, and others who lived in the mix of woodland and prairie between the Missouri and Arkansas Rivers, shared a fondness for the lotus plant, both roots and seeds. Ethnobotanist Kelly Kindscher, in his book *Edible Wild Plants of the Prairie*, said that American lotus, *Nelumbo lutea*, was highly prized and that it was considered to be invested with mystic powers by the Omahas and other Missouri River tribes. Kindscher said the hard seeds were shelled and used with meat for making soup. The tubers, after being peeled, were cut up and cooked with meat or with hominy and contributed a delicious flavor unlike any other. Kindscher also pointed out that the popularity of the plant led to overharvesting, adding that it's quite likely that the Indians propagated American lotus to the limits of its range here in the prairie bioregion.

At nearly 20 percent, lotus provides a good source of protein. The

Of Morning Haze and Lotus Flowers

seeds produce a healthy oil, and natural food websites insist that even the half-ripe seeds are tasty either raw or cooked and have a flavor similar to chestnuts. According to online recipes, the root is sweet and tasty when eaten raw, stir-fried, or served much like a sweet potato. Kindscher said Indians often used the starchy roots as a base ingredient for making their version of meat stew. The popularity of the plant extends worldwide, even though only two species exist: the Asian lotus with pink flowers and the pale yellow–flowered lotus found in the Americas. Renderings of lotus flowers appear in the early art of India, Assyria, Persia, Egypt, and Greece. And lotus was considered sacred in India, while the ancient Greeks believed the flower symbolized beauty, eloquence, and fertility.

Certainly the beauty of the lotus flower helped boost its popularity. Yet for the woodland-prairie Indians of North America, the plant added nutrients to their meat-heavy diet. This easily stored food was available for gathering in summer along with other fruits and vegetables both domestic and wild, including corn and squash planted in bottomland gardens, wild plums, and *Liatris* roots dug from upland prairies.

Osage women of old, on their way to harvest lotus tubers, would have approved of the natural bounty provided by a rainy growing season. This year, ample spring rains have left blackberry canes laden with soon-to-ripen red and already ripened black fruit. Hot, humid summers like this one can produce berries that are incredibly sweet yet still have that patent blackberry tartness. The ripe ones fall into the hand at a touch. At the same time, record rainfall has kept the grass green and the wildflowers vibrant. Patches of *Liatris*, commonly called gayfeather or blazing star, rise waist high and are topped with a clublike extension of flowers as vibrantly purple as the lotus flowers are pastel. Some species yield edible roots, others have for centuries been gathered for medicinal properties.

Compass plant is flowering in long rows, its leaves deeply lobed and more than a foot long. A native hibiscus, rosemallow, brightens the shade of a pioneering post oak that's advanced into the prairie thanks to a fox squirrel with wanderlust. Some of the rosemallow flower stems are three feet long. The flowers themselves are snow white with wine-colored centers. The actual seed-producing parts are on a projection jutting from the center like a baby's tiny white finger, each sprinkled with purple spots. This native hibiscus is a showy flower, big around as a coffee mug. And while a great number of domesticated hibiscus from other continents grace countless urban lawns, none in my estimation has the elegance of the one that grows naturally at the edge of our remaining prairielands.

Today most of the activity in this languid wetland scene arrives courtesy of butterflies, dragonflies, and damselflies. The pale blue eastern pondhawk dragonflies seem everywhere at once, their aerial gymnastics intensifying as the morning warms. The males are pretty, but I'm more inclined to admire the females, elegantly subdued with their green thoraxes and striped abdomens. Their dragonfly green matches the marsh plants dominating the insects' moist surroundings, here where cattails and arrowhead plants have a competitive edge on the upland plants that must make do with drier soils. A female pondhawk, perched on a green cattail stem, is well camouflaged and much more invested in longevity than the encircling boys in blue. The males' noticeability translates to a tasty morsel on the wing and, as dragonfly evolution dictates, certainly leaves them more expendable.

Blue is a color that finds favor in the aquatic insect world. Least bluets, damselflies shorter and thinner than a toothpick, sport a rich marine blue exterior among the males. The females, fortunately for them and for the species, range from pale gray to brown, sensible colors for the sex charged with keeping the lotus pond assured of a bluet future. While blue, green, or blue and green combos make a noticeable fashion statement among a number of dragonfly species, the more lackluster the females, the more left to survive and reproduce. As long as a single male can mate with more than one female, the guy dragonflies will remain colorful, hyperactive, and at risk.

Eastern amberwing females seem too bright for the dragonfly establishment in their blend of orange and butterscotch brown, the overall color almost metallic in bright summer sunlight. Yet the females literally pale beside the males, whose amber wings seem to glow like the light show at a music concert. The color of the male amberwing is the rich red-brown of the finest honey, illuminated by some strange sort of inner electric intensity. Amberwings aren't big dragonflies, but they are among the most beautiful. Plus they seem fond of lotus marshes, where they fit in perfectly with the overall color scheme and would do justice to etchings left on the wall of any Greek or Egyptian temple.

On a bright and fecund summer day such as this one, Osage gatherers could have filled their plaited baskets with more than lotus tubers, wild plums, blackberries, and *Liatris* roots. Arrowhead plants are flowering in the mucky shallows of the lotus pond, while Jerusalem artichokes paint the woodland edges yellow. Arrowhead, also called duck potato, is named for the big arrowhead-shaped leaves that grow in the muck inland from the lotus plants. The white flowers with yellow centers bloom along a stem that grows a foot tall or more and appears to be as stout as a stalk of celery. Waterfowl and mammals including muskrats make a meal of its seeds and tubers. Lewis and Clark, according to their journals, learned of the root's tastiness from Indians, roasted one to see for themselves, and compared the flavor to that of the common potato.

Some ethnobotanists speculate that Native Americans not only gathered but may even have cultivated the sunflower *Helianthus tuberosus*, commonly known as Jerusalem artichoke. Again, they've been compared favorably tastewise to the familiar Irish potato (actually a South American native). The post oaks bordering Pond Creek have, this wet and humid July, a bright yellow garland of Jerusalem artichokes along the edge of the woods, growing from two to six feet or more tall. According to folklore, wild pigs love to root for the tubers. However, there's no evidence that, for now, the despised feral hogs increasingly decimating wild plants throughout the region have been digging here. Sadly, it's most likely just a matter of time, as pigs gone wild join a long list of other invaders that are increasingly destroying the biological integrity of what remains of the tallgrass. The earliest of the invading exotics, commonly known as transplanted Europeans, ate Jerusalem artichokes when they were forced to, but they complained of flatulence. Unfortunately, four-legged hogs don't seem to be much bothered by gas.

It's easy to get discouraged when people introduce pests into this remnant of a landscape that at one time stretched from Canada to the Gulf of Mexico. It's even more discouraging to watch these pests, set free with no natural checks and balances, spread throughout and eventually take over native habitats, while indigenous plants and animals get pushed aside. But on this particular late July morning, there's a flash of orange in the air, a fluttering heartthrob of positivity that makes it difficult to cling to depressing thoughts.

Fritillary butterflies are in flight, both variegated and gulf species, the latter a long-winged butterfly so brightly orange, silver, and black that even nonenthusiasts tend to say "oh wow" when they spot their first one. The attraction summoning the butterflies appears to be a healthy bloom of passionflowers. Passionflower acts as a host plant for fritillary caterpillars. Gulf fritillaries seek purple passionflower or maypop, *Passiflora incarnata*, exclusively, while the smaller, less brightly colored variegated fritillary uses passionflower plus other plants.

This morning a hedgerow-like tangle of purple passionflower, along with blackberry canes, giant ragweed, a low-growing mint known as germander, and the bluish and red-tinted stems of big bluestem, all provide an early attraction for both species of fritillaries. Variegated fritillaries are either on the ground, sunning or puddling in damp earth for needed minerals, or actively seeking mates in flight. As the morning warms, these less conspicuous fritillaries seem to be everywhere.

The gulf fritillaries are less common but more noticeable. They're bigger, with longer, slimmer wings that have a bit of a boomerang shape. Males are patrolling on the wing, looking for mates, and females have come to the passionflowers, where they'll lay their eggs. The result will be a bright orange caterpillar with stiff black hairs. Bright orange in butterflies is a universal warning: I don't taste good! Some species like monarchs feed on milkweed plants and take on chemicals that can make predators nauseous. Other species simply borrow the bright orange color and derive a vicarious benefit.

On this late summer morning the heat is on, the humidity is high, and the fritillaries are dipping and bouncing slowly through the heavy air, like tiny bats the color of the setting sun. Their world is one of color, of tall yellow compass plant, of gold and gray ashy sunflower, of dark purple blazing star, of white rosemallow stained with a red wine blush.

The prairie grasses are reaching for the sky, some already flowering and setting seed. And in the marsh, yellow lotus flowers bloom. The poetry of their pale beauty this summer gives praise to the glories of summer rain, storms that brought lushness to the land, kept cattle fat, kept the hills green and growing. Osage women no longer come to feel with their toes for food buried in cool mud. Yet the cicadas persist, their raspy calling still a seasonal anthem. And from a lotus stem, a tiger-striped dragonfly with turquoise eyes surveys a world not much different from the Osage universe of old. Someday the women may need to come again, those eyes seem to say. Best to leave more than memories for tomorrow.

August on our southern grasslands is, on average, a time of heavy, raw heat. Rain, if it comes at all, often falls in tantalizing fits, as if practicing for the wetter days to follow in September. The heat is exhausting, and not much stirs except a few birds prowling for insects, bugs being the only life form that appears to appreciate the sweltering weight of late summer.

The eighth month, named for the Roman emperor Augustus, is a peak time for both highly visual and vocal insects. Sullen days echo the ratcheting reproductive pleas of cicadas clinging to the twigs of oak trees, their strident songs broadcasting their persistent urge to mate and then die and in doing so renew the life cycle of the species. Cruising dragonflies defend territories over pools stained olive green with algae, and daintier damselflies, many the color of the finest Persian turquoise, flutter in the shadows of streamside shrubbery.

At the same time, it's the season to witness the predatory behavior of wasps. These winged assassins feed on flower pollen and nectar, taking on the nourishment needed to hunt down and sting prey ranging from spiders the size of a child's hand to dog-day cicadas stridulating in the oaks like a concert of jackhammers busily busting up concrete.

After locating prey, several species of hunting wasps sting their victim in such a way that leaves the insect paralyzed but not dead. The ability to insert a stinger and inject a paralysis-producing agent seems a rather remarkable accomplishment for something as visually unremarkable as a wasp. The wasp's surgical and chemical precision in immobilizing prey results in a meal soon to be stored with wasp eggs in a tiny tunnel dug by the female. It's a macabre solution to the problem of providing fresh food for the larvae when they hatch. They'll enter the world with sustenance waiting, nourishment that can't escape and will remain alive until the brood feeds deeply enough to kill it. Evolution has provided the adult female with a way to get around the need for refrigeration at the peak of summer, and entomologists are left with a chilling life history scenario befitting a B-rated horror movie.

That's why, on a hot and humid afternoon along a prairie stream, temperature 98 degrees Fahrenheit, cicada killer wasps are digging burrows into a narrow strip of bare dirt bordering a long algae-stained pool in Hominy Creek. Cicada killers are big wasps, some nearly two inches long, and this is their time of the year and their kind of weather. They're stimulated to hunt by the buzzing din of cicadas blasting from streamside trees and shrubs. When the burrows are finished, the female wasps go on patrol. And the droning cicadas, as big as a man's thumb from tip to first joint, sing even more loudly as the temperature rises, lustily unaware of the fate that might soon befall them.

The patch of bare dirt beside the stream proves to be prime for digging birth chambers. Several wasps have settled here to burrow furiously as they prepare the nurseries that will help ensure a cicada killer future. A saltwater spill from a nearby oil field injection well erased all vegetation several years before, leaving an ugly scar. But it's a maternity ward in the making for cicada killers. These stout wasps with their rusty red heads and thoraxes, clear reddish wings, and heavy black and yellow striped abdomens are all business as the August afternoon swelters. Their own reproductive urges are equal to, yet much quieter than, those of the cicadas. The dog-day droning sounds both monotonous and at times earsplitting, the chorus cranking up to its highest volume as the late summer sun climbs heavenward.

It hasn't rained in weeks, and dry dirt kicked out of the hole by an industrious female wasp preparing her nursery chamber shoots back several feet. For a moment two females attempt to dig in the same hole, until one asserts her dominance and her rival retreats. When finished, the birth chamber will angle down six to ten inches deep by half an inch wide.

Within minutes, the female cicada killer has finished digging her hole and gone airborne, focusing her search on what will prove to be some cicada's death song. Then comes the sting with the venom that paralyzes but doesn't kill. The next step is the arduous process of dragging the victim to a place in a tree or shrub where the wasp, toting the cicada's bulk, can deliver her prey in a rapidly descending flight to a point as near to the freshly dug burrow as possible.

The cicada is then sealed within the tunnel, along with an egg laid by this hot afternoon's highly efficient hunter. In a few days the egg will hatch, and the larva will dine on the immobilized prey while the victim remains alive longer than one might anticipate. In a few more days, its nourishment reduced to little more than a shell, the young wasp will push its way out of the tunnel, well fortified and ready to assume the business of becoming some other cicada's worst nightmare.

The role of the smaller male wasps is much less dramatic and certainly less labor intensive. Male cicada killers can't sting and serve mostly to reproduce. It is the highly focused solitary females that have refined the ritual of renewing the species. And when the weather heats up and the days seem to drag themselves from sunup to sundown, these tough hunters prove that they've earned the right to claim this patch of streamside dirt as a proper nursery.

Despite the predatory efforts of cicada killer wasps, the seemingly ubiquitous dog-day cicadas survive in numbers sufficient to provide August with its own unique voice. Males utilize noisemaking portions of their exoskeletons called tymbals to flood the landscape with resonating—and sometimes nearly insufferable—mating appeal.

A short walk along the creek bank flushes dozens of the unwieldy insects from clumps of willow and buttonbush. At first they seem too cumbersome to fly, but in fact they manage quite well as long as their flights are short ones. With a flash of silver-white, a revved-up and nerve-penetrating buzz, and the flutter of cellophane wings, the cicada is away to a safer singing post.

Dog-day cicadas are referred to as annual cicadas, but actually the nymphs take from two to five years to mature. Unlike periodical cicadas, the broods aren't synchronized, with some adults emerging every year. The handsomely patterned wailing males, around $1\frac{5}{8}$ by $1\frac{1}{2}$ inches, summon females that, after mating, deposit eggs in a slit made in a tree branch. Newly hatched cicadas drop down and go underground, where they feed on tree root sap until ready to emerge. In time the rotund tenors shed a tough exoskeleton and fly out into a humid, sun-drenched world to repeat the cycle, unaware that cicada killer wasps will be waiting as they dig their hot, dry tunnels along the banks of prairie streams.

By late summer, insect appetites can leave even lightly grazed, well-watered grassland in tatters. A walk through waist-high grasses results in an orthopteran eruption as grasshoppers clinging to plant stems—stridulating, hopping, sailing, and chewing away like tiny lawn mowers—present themselves in a variety of sizes, shapes, and colors. Close inspection of ragged leaves on various forbs and grasses reveals that the insects have consumed enough plant material to play a prominent role in shaping their environment, a task they have taken seriously since as far back in history as the Carboniferous period. Grasshoppers can eat as much as half their weight in plant material daily. And in a hot, sunny, and maybe just a little extra-dry grassland, there can be an amazing number of grasshoppers.

The 1950s, a time of drought throughout the southern prairies, seemed to produce more grasshoppers than grass. The landscape snapped, crackled, and popped with grasshoppers as the insects bounded away at every step. As kids we walked to our favorite creek banks or fishing ponds, catching grasshoppers for bait along the way. The task was as easy as picking ripe fruit, and all the while we cautioned each other not to let our captives "spit tobacco juice" as they struggled. The insects actually did an ample amount of spewing a brown liquid that folklore claimed to be tobacco juice. This defensive act, an attempt to persuade predators to release the grasshoppers in favor of a more appetizing snack, did little to save them from being impaled on a fish-hook. Overall, grasshoppers tend to become prey more often than not. Considering just the numbers of prairie birds that nourish themselves and their nestlings on grasshoppers, it would appear that the best survival mechanism available to the grasshopper clan, other than spit, is their ability to reproduce in incredible numbers.

According to the *Field Guide to Grasshoppers, Katydids, and Crickets of the United States*, grasshoppers belong to the order Orthoptera, a group that also includes crickets and katydids. Orthoptera translates to "straight wings," but some believe that the order would be better named for the insects' massive thighs and the jumping prowess such well-developed thighs enable. A field biologist once postulated that if a grasshopper was as large as a human being, the distance covered during an average leap would be around the length of a football field.

There are thousands of species of grasshoppers around the world, and most are generalists in their dining habits. Some prefer grass, some prefer broad-leaved plants, but very few dine on only a single species of anything. Such blue-collar tastes contribute to healthy populations that tend to outbreak at times with devastating results. Generally, however, grasshoppers remain a successful species by not eating themselves out of existence, good news for all the species (including some tribes of *Homo sapiens*) that depend upon the 50 to 75 percent protein that their carcasses provide. A grassland bereft of grasshoppers would be a very hungry place for prairie-chickens, turkey, quail, and meadowlarks, plus all the other species that raise nestlings to maturity on this nutritious food source.

Back in the not-so-good old days, enormous aggregations of grasshoppers sometimes assembled, took on certain physical characteristics that would allow for mass migration, then launched an overland odyssey that laid waste to most anything chewable that lay in the ravenous assemblage's path. These clouds of migratory grasshoppers, numbering in the billions, maybe trillions, were known as locusts. Probably the most famous locust swarm was the biblical horde that helped Moses and his tribe part company with an Egyptian pharaoh in Old Testament times.

Closer to home and as recently as 1875, the dreaded Rocky Mountain locust ate its way across the American heartland in swarms that were estimated to be 1,800 miles long and 110 miles wide. In terms of square miles, this eruption devastated a swath of land larger than the state of California. Considering that these swarms were basically a solid mass of insects that blocked out the sun as they migrated, the 1875 outbreak contained an almost inconceivable amount of insect appetites. They ate crops, grass, the paint off barns. Women who covered their gardens with blankets watched in horror as the grasshoppers ate the blankets on their way to consuming the tender plants beneath.

Laura Ingalls Wilder in *On the Banks of Plum Creek* described a locust swarm thusly: "The cloud was hailing grasshoppers. The cloud *was* grasshoppers. Their bodies hid the sun and made darkness. Their thin, large wings gleamed and glittered. The rasping whirring of their wings filled the whole air and they hit the ground and the house with the noise of a hailstorm."

According to witnesses, locust swarms like the one Wilder described could literally clean a farmer out of house and home, achieving "total consumption: crops, fabric or clothing. Farmers tried in vain to fight the swarms with fires and metal scoops covered with tar or molasses, and were met with destruction on a catastrophic scale." As reported in *Wild West Magazine*, "the locusts soon scoured the fields of crops, the trees of leaves, every blade of grass, the wool off sheep, the harnesses off horses, the paint off wagons, the handles off pitchforks—the locusts, farmers grimly quipped, 'ate everything but the mortgage.'"

Fortunately for western agriculture, the Rocky Mountain locust vanished from the planet shortly after the turn of the twentieth century. The western river bottoms that the insects favored for egg laying were converted to agricultural cropland, and one of North America's most terrifying spectacles of nature soon disappeared as a consequence. It's mystifying to consider that a species capable of migrations encompassing billions of individuals and laying waste to thousands of square miles became extinct so quickly, but it did.

The life of a grasshopper begins in the soil that it will return to rather quickly, either as a grasshopper that's completed its life cycle or as excrement from a bird, a mammal, or another insect that has ingested a grasshopper in hopes of prolonging a life cycle of its own. Following mating, female grasshoppers deposit clusters of eggs, from as few as four to more than a hundred, in the soil. Eggs are laid in a frothy secretion that hardens to provide protection for the cluster.

Most eggs are laid in autumn, overwinter, then hatch in the spring.

The nymphs then mature through the growing season, molting as many as half a dozen exteriors as they progress. By the time of the final molt, the grasshopper is equipped with mature wings and sex organs. In the north, these adults mate, lay eggs, and then face the end of their first and only glorious summer of grasshopper existence. In the south, however, both adults and nymphs may overwinter and even be active on warm sunny days.

The basic working parts of a grasshopper include the head, thorax, and abdomen. The thorax includes a shieldlike dorsal covering known as the pronotum. Attached to the thorax are three pairs of legs. The hind legs include the massive femurs that provide for the grasshopper tribe's legendary leaping ability and may include markings or color combinations that help ascertain species lineage. At the terminus of all these legs is a multisegmented footlike structure known as a tarsus.

The legs of some species may include spines that aid in self-defense. Also attached to the thorax are the wings, which may be long in some species, short in others, or little more than rudimentary pads. All grasshoppers come equipped with tough mandibles, perfect for rendering plant tissue into digestible pieces.

The demise of the Rocky Mountain locust doesn't mean that modern-day grasshoppers don't respond to environmental stimuli and eat with the intensity of insect grim reapers upon occasion. Sue Selman, friend and owner of a native grass cattle ranch in northwest Oklahoma, remembers the grasshopper swarms that infested her place during the drought-ridden 1950s. The insects, she said, quickly ate all the plants around her home. Then when all the vegetation was gone, the grasshoppers helped themselves to all the paint on her house and outbuildings.

During a prolonged grassland drought, it seems that the entire universe is made up of these multicolored and multishaped insects that leap like the most agile of amphibians and eat with equine appetites. In the hot sun of a dry prairie summer, the land literally crackles with grasshoppers, even though grassland birds consume them with enthusiasm and feed their young little else when the insects are abundant. Such massive amounts of protein appeal not only to birds but to mammalian appetites and other insects as well.

Before farmer and plow converted the majority of America's prairies to domestic cropland, migrants winging their way to the Arctic feasted upon clusters of grasshopper eggs buried in shallow soil. Con-

A Few Thoughts about Aesop's Favorite Loafer

jecture has it that the great flocks of Eskimo curlews once depended upon America's native prairies and their grasshopper egg buffet to fuel spring migration. Grasshoppers still can and do swell to astounding numbers when the weather turns hot and dry. Unfortunately hot, dry grasslands generally mean fiscal tough times for ranchers attempting to stretch their native forage to a profitable margin. As a result, higher education in entomology may mean more emphasis on eradicating grasshoppers than on understanding their highly evolved role in a functioning prairie ecosystem.

A SEASON SPUN IN GOLD

At times in late September, it seems that the prairie is mostly made of spiderwebs. A sunrise drenched with dew illuminates jeweled strands, each strung with liquid silver pearls, stretching from grass stalk to grass stalk. The largest webs are the handiwork of the big garden spiders, the black and yellow and banded *Argiope* spiders big as a sparrow's egg, each richly patterned with handsome silver, black, and yellow bands and lines.

These large spiders spin a round web that's some two feet in diameter. The male, much smaller than the female and more interested in mating than anything else, builds a less elaborate web nearby that's minuscule in comparison to the female's grand achievement. Every night, the matriarch *Argiope* consumes her web and rebuilds the circular interior with fresh silk. Generally, the frame and anchor lines are left in place, while the rest goes back into the builder for recycling.

September's dewy sunrise glow also reveals the functional artwork of grass spiders. These smaller arachnids build dense sheet webs that glisten near the ground, webs that look like a patch of loosely woven cloth when saturated with dew. Grass spider webs aren't as neat and orderly as *Argiope* webs, but still a prey insect that miscalculates and flies headlong into a sheet web better have some trustworthy escape moves. Grass spiders are the Olympic sprinters of spiderwebdom, and it's rare that prey can become disentangled before the spider arrives to administer a paralyzing bite.

Late September, during those days around the autumn equinox, is prime spider renewal time on the tallgrass prairie. Spiders, along with a variety of other insect species, are busily preparing for the final generation of the season. The grasslands are literally abuzz with insects driven either to lay a last round of eggs and then die or to overwinter as adults, reemerge in the spring, and launch a new generation. Whatever the procreative sequence, September arrives on the wings of insect multitudes, many of which reach the end of their days encased in spider silk, wrapped as neatly as a pork chop from a grocery counter.

Around the third week of September, the days are once again nearly equal, daylight and dark. The lessening amount of sunlight is a signal to a number of species, spelling out the need to complete any business at hand before frost arrives. In the southern tallgrass country, the average first freeze comes in late October, leaving a lot of bugs with only a few short weeks to finish up their annual business of providing for an upcoming generation.

Fortunately, the season of the autumn equinox can at times seem springlike, providing excellent weather for passing genes along to the next generation. Some spring flowers are blooming again, birds and animals are on the move, nights are comfortable, and weather fronts oftentimes bring blessed rainfall.

The most noticeable difference between May and late September is the color. The autumn equinox is a season of smoky gold, of copper and bronze pressed against crisp blue skies. The bright greens predominating early in the growing season have shifted to earth tones, presenting a homespun canvas enlivened by yellow, turquoise, and purple flowers, including asters, salvias, late-flowering members of the sunflower tribe, and of course goldenrod.

Goldenrod may be the most striking of September's yellow varieties. Few flowers are more aptly named or more adapted to native grasslands than this autumn insect favorite. Goldenrod, laden with pollen, nourishes monarch butterflies on their long migratory flight to Mexico. Late in September, pastures overgrown with goldenrod once erupted with monarchs lifting skyward like a burst of orange flame, fortified and ready to flutter south to the Texas Gulf Coast and then continue a long flight across the gulf to Mexico.

Upon close inspection, you'll find that many flowering goldenrod plants are crawling with soldier beetles. These insects, slim and about an inch long, blend in well due to their butterscotch brown and black wing covers. Adult soldier beetles are fond of dining on aphids, the tiny sap-feeding insects found on the leaves of native prairie plants. But soldier beetles also favor pollen and nectar, so hanging out on goldenrod satisfies several appetites. Here they'll have a chance to devour aphids, then follow up with goldenrod pollen for dessert. Also, the goldenrod season is prime for mating. Afterward the female lays her clutch of eggs in the soil, where they'll hatch the following spring.

For all its beauty, goldenrod is often accused of being the plant that initiates the fitful sneezing, coughing, and bloodshot eyes of autumn's allergy season. In fact, the main culprit in prairie country is annual or common ragweed, a plant easily overlooked but a dispenser of potent pollen in copious amounts. Goldenrod gets accused because it's widespread and calls attention to itself through its eye-catching floral display. Common ragweed, on the other hand, grows low to the ground and flowers inconspicuously. It also invades disturbed areas, allowing for ragweed pollen indexes that often top the charts in late summer and early autumn. On the brighter side, ragweed seeds provide a plentiful plant food coveted by native birds. It may not be much consolation, but the weeks of misery endured by allergy sufferers are, in some ways, offset by a bountiful pantry open to feathered benefactors, including bobwhite quail.

Early in October, persimmons the size of golf balls are beginning to ripen on trees mostly barren of leaves now that annual seed-bearing chores are behind them. The fruit will be ready for consumption following the first freeze. That's when the bitter taste fades and persimmon-loving mammals begin redistributing the large reddish brown seeds within the fiber-rich orange fruit. As soon as the fruit is ripe, the oval seeds begin to appear in all sorts of scat across the prairie. White-tailed deer stand on their hind legs to reach ripe persimmons, coyotes savor them like candy, and raccoon do their best to outconsume the competition. Seeds of this nutritious soft mast achieve mobility courtesy of four legs on the prowl, tagging along internally as their benefactor rambles. Sooner or later they'll drop back to the soil, fertilizer included, doing what a persimmon seed does best to open up new persimmon horizons.

Other trees and shrubs employ similar strategies for seed dispersal. Sumac bushes turn bright crimson early in autumn, when the rust-colored seed clusters are ready for consumption. Walnut trees turn yellow and drop their leaves early to reveal nuts still in their leathery green husks. Neighborhood fox and gray squirrels aren't picky about green husks or the edibility of prefrost acorns. They go after the newly formed nuts with gusto. The sound of multiple squirrels chewing away at early pecans, acorns, and walnuts provides the season with gritty percussion to back up late bursts of birdsong.

Late September prairie streams are swirling with vernal activity as well. Pools may swarm with red shiner minnows, beautiful creatures some two inches long, the males' bluish silver scales and bright red fins flashing like beacons during the breeding season. Small crayfish dart from rock to rock, seeking cover. At times the pools are encircled by stands of cattails or prairie cordgrass or both, the elongated stems serving as perches for meadowhawk dragonflies.

Some of the meadowhawks have red abdomens, contrasting with the slimmer, daintier metallic blue of damselflies sunning streamside. The meadowhawks, even the red ones, aren't as flashy as many of the dragonfly species, yet few share their tenacity. Meadowhawks fly late into the year. You'll see them active on moderately warm days as late as December. They tend to fly over open grassland in swarms in late summer and early autumn, cruising low, maneuvering with dazzling speed. The scene's not complete until hundreds of these dragonflies are darting and circling over a patch of prairie about the size of a school playground. Then it's easy to believe that dragonflies really do dance. It's an aerial ballet that's almost magical, especially at the end of an autumn day, with the setting sun illuminating thousands of opaque silver wings flashing like tiny mirrors.

Southern leopard frogs, seemingly missing in action since the frenetic days and nights of early spring's breeding season, suddenly appear to be everywhere by late September. Tasks foremost on a leopard frog's autumn schedule include staying alive, growing as fat as possible, and finding a good spot to overwinter.

Unfortunately for these brown-spotted amphibians, not many carnivores reject a meal of fresh frog legs. Few scenes are more riveting than a black rat snake swallowing a leopard frog, the frog screaming almost like a human child as it slowly descends into the snake's midsection through unhinged and distended jaws, the snake calmly partaking of lunch by moving the object of its appetite inward via muscular contraction. It's a scene of pure horror for those with a psychological aversion to snakes, and people are quick to club the snake to rescue the frog, a reaction that explains why those being preyed upon tend to be both loud and shrill when their fate coincides with a snake's supper.

Of course there are cool overcast days as well, with fronts bringing thunderstorms followed by overnight lows in the forties. Gray skies make for solemn days, the chirping of field crickets adding to the melancholy. At times the crickets compete with the clucking of turkey, the latter calling loudly while scratching away at grass and leaf litter as they search for acorns.

Breaks in the clouds allow shafts of sunlight to illuminate the dense clumps of sunflowers that dominate this period of nearly equal day and night. Late September sunflowers provide the purest gold of the prairie's golden season, the robust flowers swaying in the wind to cricket and turkey background music.

At least one of several sunflower species is usually blooming from July through the end of October. Common or annual sunflowers, the tallest of the tribe with their stout stalks and big fan-shaped leaves, seem to be everywhere. These annuals sprout each year from the previous year's seed and favor disturbed soil. By late autumn they're joined by several perennial species, including Maximilian sunflowers with boatlike leaves and vivid butter yellow flowers. Willowleaf sunflowers, not as common, favor late September limestone outcrops where the flowers grow in colonies on stems covered with whorled leaves.

The perennial sunflowers have evolved as part of the tallgrass prairie tapestry. Nutritious and eagerly sought for grazing forage as well as for their fruit, sunflowers provide a source of seed that helps sustain wintering birds and small mammals. To the uninitiated, they're just weeds invading grass meant for cattle. Yet for wildlife, sunflowers are manna from heaven.

BUTTERFLY SUMMER

A few days following the summer solstice, a prairie hay meadow near the Kansas-Oklahoma state line filled with orchids. Back in May, it had been a vast pale purple field of wild hyacinths. Then near the end of June, the bright green meadow erupted in low white orchids, unique in the way that the small flowers encircled the stalk, spiraling around the stem like the stripe on a barber's pole.

Ladies' tresses orchids aren't showy plants. Yet they're structurally remarkable and rarely as common as those I found growing during the wet spring of 2015. The summer of this El Niño year produced flooding throughout the region and removed any lingering counties from the regional drought map. Frequent rains kept the climate uncharacteristically humid, while temperatures along the Kansas-Oklahoma line remained below the hundred-degree mark throughout the summer. Yet even though the temperatures remained cooler than average, July and August days were sometimes sweltering due to high dew points. Essentially it was grass-growing weather, perfect for producing fat cattle and plenty of bugs.

Early in July, buttonbush began to flower along the banks of Sand Creek, a tributary of the Caney River. A beautiful section of this stream is protected in Oklahoma's Osage Hills State Park, including a stretch of sandstone bedrock where the creek splashes over a series of low waterfalls.

Buttonbush tends to grow thickly through cracks in the sandstone here, and on a hot, calm July morning its white flowers, round and nearly as big as golf balls, were swarming with pipevine swallowtail butterflies. Dozens of bright neon blue and black insects circled the plants, flashing vivid orange spots concealed under their wings. These swallowtails were big butterflies and colorful, powerful fliers. However, their easily overlooked companions were anything but. Buttonbush flowers also appeared to be a magnet for numerous silver-spotted skippers, none of them much bigger than the tip of a man's thumb. These tiny butterflies sipped nectar with their wings folded like little jet fighter planes grounded by foul weather. The skipper color scheme, compared to the flashiness of the swallowtails, was subdued yet tasteful—dark brown wings bearing orange windows, along with a prominent white or silver spot.

For several weeks that summer, both variegated and gulf fritillaries dominated the place where the passionflowers grew near the mouth of Birch Creek, a small prairie stream. Variegated fritillaries were tastefully handsome in their orange and black color scheme, an eye-catching insect showy enough for the passionflower extravaganza providing the attraction. The gulf fritillaries, on the other hand, were almost magical. Their longer, slimmer wings hinted at something bird- or batlike, while the color of their wings mirrored that of a glowing red-orange rising sun. Upper wing surfaces were streaked with stylistic black lines and scattered black spots. The butterflies' lower wings sported small silver panes that glowed like stained glass with each beat.

Fritillaries and friends enjoyed a floral smorgasbord that splendid summer growing season, including an extended flowering period for the passionflowers. Prairie openings soon filled with the rich purple hues of *Liatris*, or prairie blazing star, a butterfly favorite. And from midsummer through most of October, the grasses were tinted yellow by both the sunflower and the *Silphium* tribes.

The yellow season started with golden blooms atop the coarse stalks and foliage of compass plant and rosinweed. By the time the meadows were daubed with purple patches of *Liatris*, ashy, Maximilian, and common sunflowers had joined the mix. Rounding out this flood of nectar providers were milky white mallows and, as a last hurrah, a burst of golden bidens appeared near the end of the growing season. All this nectar on the stem drew butterflies of every size, hue, and description, with the final round flying into November. That's when orange fiery skippers visited hardy asters along with yellow sulphurs both large and small. Unfortunately, the butterflies that usually dominate the end of summer on the southern prairie remained elusive, noticeably so. The monarchs seemed to be missing.

As recently as twenty years ago, I'd watched September skies over the Arkansas River fill with uncountable monarch butterflies journeying southward, some fluttering along in undulating flight at treetop height, others barely visible pinpoints of orange, surging irresistibly toward Mexico at the same altitude as circling bald eagles.

At times in the past, there seemed to be so many of these handsome insects that it was impossible to imagine that a day might come when this autumn spectacle would be history. But September of 2015, my first back in the tallgrass country following three years in the Southwest, offered only occasional sightings of monarch groups, with these rarely numbering more than five or six. By the end of the month, I was worriedly driving every day to some point far out in the prairie where I had previously seen thousands of monarchs on overnight roosts. But the trees were bare, and the skies remained empty.

I checked notes I'd collected over the years, dating back to the mid-1980s. They indicated that by the end of September, Osage County should be inundated with monarchs. The first entry, dated September 28 more than thirty years ago, began "butterflies abound." It noted that the migration was growing stronger by the day, with migrants dropping from the skies to visit flowering goldenrod.

The second entry, dated September 29, 1989, commented on violent storms with ample rain arriving on the heels of a front that dropped the high temperature twenty degrees to a more moderate seventy. The journal page entry read, "Monarch migration strong today. Not many butterflies in the oak timber, since they aren't stopping to rest or visit flowers. Mostly you see them along the higher ridges, where the wind blows them quickly south. Thousands pass in front of me as I drive down the highway, with many killed by cars. I see numerous butterflies 'mudding' at roadside potholes or in the soft mud of county dirt roads. The monarchs seem to be blown along, more than flying."

On September 29, this time in 1996, my journal notes once again mentioned a wind blowing from the north, with an overnight low of 40 degrees. "Skies filled with migrating monarchs," the entry proclaimed. "The butterflies seem especially fond of goldenrod, and in places the bright golden flowers are covered with the insects, each butterfly holding tight as the stalks whip back and forth in the wind. Also, lots of monarchs dropping down to visit blazing star."

Later that evening, according to my notes, the "monarchs landed in a Shumard oak tree and a pecan growing in the center of an open field. The following morning the butterflies were still hanging like clustered leaves from the tips of branches, the temperature still too cool for the insects to continue their migration. Finally, after the rising sun broke over the tops of the trees and warmed the fragile travelers, they began to depart, one by one."

The entries continued: "September 28, 2003, Pawhuska, Oklahoma. Monarchs arriving on a north wind. Now and then one alights on some wildflower to refuel. A beautiful sight, the bright orange butterflies visiting the turquoise blue salvia, all mixed in with the golden seed sprays of Indiangrass."

And on September 24, 2006: "Fairfax, Oklahoma. Migrating monarch butterflies thick along the little creek bordering Fairfax cemetery. Hundreds have spent the night in the big cottonwoods and pecans growing there. The butterflies still haven't resumed their migration by eight the following morning. The day begins partly cloudy, cool with a strong north wind, reaching a high temperature in the mid-seventies."

The last entry, written in 2014, was still somewhat optimistic. "Stopped at the western edge of the Oklahoma panhandle, where a strong south wind has migrating monarchs grounded during the middle of the day. The butterflies wait out the windstorm in Chinese elms growing in what was an old travel trailer park in Boise City. Later in the afternoon, northeast of Pawhuska around Hulah Lake, monarch butterflies are leisurely feeding on goldenrod growing around the lakeshore. A mature bald eagle watches the butterfly show from the upper branches of a dead tree. Both goldenrod and rough blazing star flowering, offering a fulfilling bounty for the migrants."

But September 2015 slipped past without a sign of the butterflies. Then, during the first week of October on a cool cloudy morning following the arrival of a cold front, I flushed around a dozen monarchs from several tall black willow trees growing along the banks of Pond Creek, just south of the Kansas-Oklahoma line. They were roosting in the leaves and finally began to flutter out of the foliage as the morning warmed a little.

Later that day, I noticed an online report by several birders who'd visited a wetland in southwest Oklahoma, both to look for migrant shorebirds and to check out a monarch roost area on a small lake. Their report noted that "in 2008 around this date we observed thousands of Monarchs roosting in the clump of trees just east of the reservoir and on the same side of the road. Yesterday evening in the same spot, at 6:45 PM, we saw 100 butterflies."

The monarch migration is a resolute march, a journey made by some of earth's frailest creatures starting as far north as Canada, then moving south across the Gulf of Mexico and deep into the mountains of Mexico. That's a dangerous journey for a migrating bird, while a monarch most likely wouldn't equal the weight of a goose's wing feather. At times it seems that the butterflies are blown south—on a windy day, the monarchs dip and flutter like autumn leaves when buffeted by the wind. Yet they struggle on, not to be denied, until the lucky ones arrive safely at their wintering grounds in Mexico.

A grove of post oak trees grew just west of my childhood home, and in the evening during the peak of the monarch migration the grove would fill up with butterflies settling in for the night. Just before dark, this grove and others scattered throughout the prairie would be covered with a solid mass of monarchs, and as the sun set they would fan their wings in unison. As a result, the dusty dull green of the oaks would suddenly flash vivid orange in the waning light. The pulsing continued, orange to dull green, then back to orange, until it was too dark to see. For a boy of ten or twelve, it was pure magic.

Early in the morning during the migration peak, I would walk half a mile to a neighboring rancher's horse pasture, one mostly grown up in flowering goldenrod. Monarchs by the thousands were on or just above the bright yellow flowers, as if an orange and black fog had settled over the land. As I watched, the butterflies streamed from the goldenrod patches to join with butterflies already overhead, forming a procession that pressed slowly yet steadily toward the Texas coast.

What's left of our monarchs may spend as many as forty-seven to ninety days covering some 2,800 miles during migration. And all the while, these butterflies making their autumn flight have no physical knowledge of the destination they seek—they were born during the spring migration, hatching from eggs laid by overwintering adults that died soon after. Newborn monarchs continue the northward flight, following the spring resurrection of the milkweed plants vital to their survival. Several generations continue to mate, reproduce, and die before the final generation reaches adulthood and returns to Mexico to renew the process. How this final generation understands when and where to migrate remains a mystery.

The scientific community didn't even know the location of the Mexican winter roost near Michoacán until 1976, when the site was revealed in an article published in *National Geographic*. It's a wonderful place for the butterflies to overwinter but a perilous place due to the human factor—the timber resources the monarchs utilize on that mountain slope also have monetary value.

In the spring the overwintering migrants leave Mexico, once again cross the gulf, and return to Texas by mid-March. Upon reaching the mainland, mated females seek the choicest milkweed plants for egg laying. These eggs hatch, and monarch larvae feed on the milkweed, mature, and then move north to complete their own generational process. As spring extends into summer, the march of these succeeding generations reaches as far north as Canada.

Key to this odyssey is the milkweed plant, including tallgrass prairie natives like antelopehorn, green, narrow-leaved, showy, and swamp milkweeds. Each new generation follows these awakening milkweeds as springtime advances. Overwintering migrants returning to Texas from Mexico will have been alive for as many as eight months, survived all the hazards of the autumn migration, and then returned to the southern United States via a 750-mile flight. After they reproduce, the bedraggled adults perish.

Monarch caterpillars are stout, voracious insects that hatch from singly laid eggs. They increase in size at an astonishing rate, growing from around two millimeters long to around three thousand times their hatching weight in two weeks. Prominently banded in contrasting yellow, black, and white, the caterpillars enter the chrysalis or pupal stage for nine to fifteen days before emerging as winged adults.

A milkweed diet provides caterpillars with chemical compounds that render the insects distasteful to many would-be predators. Adult monarchs continue to store these compounds, advertising their distastefulness with vivid colors. Successful spring migration hinges on the monarchs' ability to advance north with the maturation of the milkweed plants, concentrating on about half a dozen *Asclepias* species they hope to find in prime, chemically potent condition.

Some three generations of monarchs will hatch, mature, lay up to five hundred eggs, and die before the spring advance reaches its terminal northern breeding range in southern Ontario. Peak concentrations during the spring migration occur in the Upper Midwest, where some 50 percent of the autumn migrants originate.

Each monarch generation is superbly equipped for life in search of the perfect milkweed. The insects have large wings that, according to the scientists who study them, supply excellent lift-to-drag ratios. Adults feed on flowers containing carbohydrates in the form of sugar-rich nectar. Males are larger than females and aggressive when it comes to tackling potential mates midflight and dragging them to the ground to complete the business of monarch procreation.

Not that long ago, substantial numbers reached the southern Flint Hills near the end of September, a time of year when cool fronts finally managed to push south, pulling temperatures down from the nineties into the seventies and bringing cool, rainy north winds with them. Cold fronts provided a tailwind but tough environmental conditions for the travelers. A severe storm could ground a flight or even destroy a percentage of it, while collisions with trucks and automobiles oftentimes left highways littered with lifeless orange and black wings.

In the spring of 2016 Monarch Watch, a butterfly conservation organization, reported that an unprecedented storm struck the monarchs' Mexican wintering grounds, uprooting trees and dumping inches of sleet that buried thousands of butterflies and left others frozen on their perches. As many as 50 percent of the butterflies that hadn't yet left for the North American prairies may have perished, and observers could only guess at the long-term toll on an already diminished population. Still, somehow, despite storms, habitat alteration, chemicals, and the perils of being a butterfly in a modern world that tends to spin too fast for them, the species manages to cling to survival. The monarch migration and its mysteries have long cast a spell that intrigues scientists and inspires emotions that approach rhapsody. But without some immediate help, this handsome sylph of pure natural magic may not be around to delight our grandchildren.

THE MOSTLY MISUNDERSTOOD COPPERHEAD

A copperhead snake really is a beautiful animal, in spite of the panic that arises at the mention of its name. *Agkistrodon contortrix* displays abstract patterns of tan, pink, gray, copper, and brown when pressed against a pale limestone outcrop. Yet the same snake becomes nearly invisible when nestled against a shady carpet of dry oak leaves. Sadly, fangs designed to envenomate and a sinister reputation generally overrule any appreciation for the reptile's classy camouflage and instead mark the animal for instant death—a fate generated more by fear than by fact and an ageless attitude toward "serpents" that too often borders on near hysteria.

Copperheads, common in the wooded rocky draws and canyons along the tallgrass prairie's waterways, seek to escape the wrath of all sorts of adversaries by remaining quietly in place and allowing a hard-to-detect hide to do the job it was designed for. Those of us who've spent a lifetime on foot in copperhead country most likely would be mortified if we knew exactly how many snakes we've nearly stepped on. Many bites occur when copperheads actually are stepped on, probably second only to the number of bites inflicted upon amateurs who can't resist handling poisonous snakes.

Fortunately for these untrained snake handlers, the copperhead's bite is rarely lethal. On the other hand, I watched a 110-pound dog grow quite ill in a matter of minutes following a single bite on a back leg by a snake so small that it didn't appear capable of killing a cotton rat, much less ruining the day of a young and healthy Labrador retriever. The dog recovered, but only after two days under the care of a veterinarian with treatment that included expensive doses of antivenin.

Some dogs, like some people, never seem to understand that snakes can pack a punch much greater than their mere inches. My black Lab Jack was as lucky as the aforementioned yellow Lab wasn't. He loved to roam with me along the broken cliffs bordering a prairie stream. It was the epitome of copperhead country—vertical slabs of stone broken by erosion and by gravity, resulting in fissures, overhangs, small caves, and an abundance of eroded rubble, a clutter of both big boulders and small.

These rocky breaks provided the communal dens preferred by copperheads, while a mix of oak-hickory woodlands both above and below the bluffs housed snakes galore during spring, summer, and autumn. The woods were crisscrossed by deer trails and carpeted with a thick layer of oak leaf mulch. Copperheads were prevalent along the game trails and, when coiled against leaf patterns including multiple shades of brown and tan, the well-camouflaged snakes were nearly impossible to detect.

Both the black Lab and I walked these trails almost every morning, and many times I either inadvertently stepped over copperheads or came within inches of stepping on them. The Lab, often lagging behind, would come upon the snake, sniff, and offer his nose at point-blank range. The copperheads, true to their advertised demeanor, never struck. Almost all simply waited, coiled and motionless, until the nosy dog and his clumsy companion wandered on down the trail before slinking away to a more secluded hideout.

Once a small copperhead, pressed by the sniffing black Lab, pulled its head back and tucked it under an oak leaf, desperate for concealment even though at least sixteen to eighteen additional inches remained in plain view. On the other hand, on a couple of warm afternoons I've had several snakes strike yet stop short of the mark, sort of a copperhead's warning shot fired across the bow. The most dramatic encounter involved a beautiful specimen exhibiting rusty red-brown hourglass bands over a background of pinkish tan. This snake was sunning on the trail following a night of cool rain, and when we came upon it unexpectedly it bolted for the nearby woods, partly elevated, striking out repeatedly to keep us at bay. I don't believe that this snake ever had any intention of biting anyone—it was simply making a strategic retreat, firing the big guns at every opportunity to keep the advancing army at bay.

Copperheads come in several subspecies and color combinations, but essentially all are the same snake with minor environmental adaptations. Sometimes the background color is tan, sometimes pinkish, sometimes brown, sometimes gray. Generally the bands are a deep chestnut to rusty brown and constricted in the middle, forming an hourglass shape or a fat figure eight. The head is plain except for the copper-colored scales on top, thus the name.

Young-of-the-year copperheads look like adults except for a yellowish tint to the tip of the tail. Some speculate that young snakes use this colored appendage much like an angler uses a brightly colored lure. The copperhead wiggles its tail, small creatures ease up to investigate, and bang! Baby copperhead has a bellyful. These small youngsters, waiting amid dried vegetation along a stream bank, are almost impossible to locate, and I've had them strike often and vigorously when I've stood too closely. Fortunately I had on sturdy leather boots, and the small snakes never actually sank a fang in them.

Copperheads are close cousins to cottonmouths, another poisonous snake found near water in more southern climes. Adult cottonmouths are generally an overall dull brown, and like copperheads they tend to remain motionless rather than flee when approached. Young cottonmouths are more brightly banded than the adults and can be mistaken for copperheads. They, too, use their sulfur yellow tail tips to lure prey.

According to the reams of literature written about snakebites (some of it scientific, some of it not), a copperhead bite is generally not fatal. Most experts urge copperhead bite recipients to seek medical attention, because "not fatal" doesn't mean you're going to escape excruciating pain and permanently marred extremities if the bites aren't treated. The severity of a snakebite seems to hinge upon a number of factors, including whether the snake actually injected venom, how much venom it injected if it did, where on the body the bite occurred, and the amount of time before the bitten party receives treatment. The best snakebite prevention remains a stout pair of high-topped boots, because no matter how closely you watch your feet, a motionless copperhead coiled against leaf litter in the shade has an evolutionary advantage.

Copperheads leave their communal dens after the danger of a hard freeze has subsided and move to more solitary hunting territory. As the weather warms, they become increasingly nocturnal. In the summer months, I've usually encountered them when they're basking in the very early morning along some trail.

However, on a mild spring day, a copperhead with an appetite can be anywhere that prey could be available. Rodents, small birds, and even insects are on the menu for these pit vipers that are, literally, armed to the teeth, even if they're not predisposed to use them.

AN OSAGE THOREAU

In the spring of 2015, the Oklahoma chapter of the Nature Conservancy announced that they'd acquired acreage to add to the organization's Tallgrass Prairie Preserve. Included within the acquisition was an old cabin built of native sandstone, circa 1932. For many years it had been the home of John Joseph Mathews, Osage historian, novelist, artist, poet, and philosopher. The sturdy old dwelling was the one he built when he decided to cut short his travels, return home after studying at Oxford and Geneva and hunting in Africa, and live in harmony with the land of his upbringing. Over the years Mathews would write five books in this simple structure, including a Book of the Month Club best seller, a prairie version of Thoreau's *Walden*, and a poetic history of the Osage tribe.

Mathews' cabin, hidden away from the road at the edge of a miniforest of blackjack oaks, had neither electricity nor running water. Heat came from a carefully designed arched fireplace also built of native stone. Mathews' daughter Virginia remembers visiting her father in the summertime and showering under a pan with a number of holes poked in the bottom, Mathews' backyard concession to cleanliness.

The cabin sits at the edge of an oak-studded ridgeline. Beyond the front door the world opens to encompass miles of rolling high prairie.

Streams have cut deep draws, and cattle drink from stock ponds filled by wet weather seeps and springs. The Nature Conservancy soon replaced the majority of the cattle grazing on the surrounding pastureland with buffalo. The bison roam freely and replicate ancient grazing patterns. Their keystone presence is part of the conservancy's mission to restore biological integrity to the preserve, the nation's largest protected tract of tallgrass prairie.

Mathews' gravesite lies near the old stone dwelling, and now bison dung rather than cow manure fertilizes the adjacent countryside. Somehow it just seems fitting that nearby blackjacks will serve as scratching posts for bison grown weary of their winter wool. Not even a visionary like John Joseph Mathews could have guessed that some-day his Osage Indian allotment would be home to an animal that the Osage people once revered, yet one that had vanished long before Mathews was born. By the time of the Osages' final buffalo hunt in the mid-1870s, only a few of the animals remained on the high plains of extreme northwest Oklahoma and southwest Kansas, and these too would soon disappear due to pressure applied by hungry Indians and a swarm of white hide hunters.

In his youth, John Joseph Mathews lived the life I often dreamed about while riding my horse not far from where he was raised. Born in Pawhuska in 1894, Mathews witnessed firsthand what some historians have labeled the last chapter of the old Wild West, a turbulent era that had grown into legend by the time I was born in 1947.

Of Osage descent, Mathews spoke the language and played with the children of Osages only recently removed from the lives of warriors and buffalo hunters. And when young John Joseph explored the rolling hills along the headwaters of Bird Creek, train robbers, whiskey run-ners, and horse thieves were still around to share a path through the rocky grassland.

Mathews roamed the prairie when the prairie-chickens still gath-ered in great flocks, when Eskimo curlews still landed to feed on greening spring pastures, and when wolves still howled from black-jack-studded caprock and cougars carried away small children—one of them his infant brother. John Joseph grew to manhood at the end of a raucous time in the region's history, a time soon to be replaced by near-total chaos courtesy of an oil boom and the environmental and cultural corruption that go hand in hand with the discovery of black gold. When he left the Osage prairie for college, service in World War

I, and time in England as a Rhodes Scholar, the departure would have been, for most, a ticket to a more sophisticated world that Mathews was quite capable of flourishing in. Yet the pull of the Osage countryside and its people remained strong. The son of a Pawhuska businessman came back to the tallgrass, built the little sandstone house, and began to reconnect with the rhythms of the land and its people.

Creatively inspired by his homecoming, Mathews began to write seriously about the region. His first book, *Wah'Kon-Tah: The Osage and the White Man's Road*, focused on the Osage tribe's removal from Kansas to its reservation in Oklahoma and the often futile attempts to "civilize" a people quite content to remain as they were. The story, told through the eyes of a sympathetic Indian agent, captures the dignity of tribal members even as their culture begins to unravel.

Wah'Kon-Tah, published by the University of Oklahoma Press in 1929, was chosen as a Book of the Month Club selection, the first-ever selection from an academic press. It became a best seller. Later Mathews would publish a novel, *Sundown*, a partly autobiographical look at a young man of mixed Osage and Anglo blood trying to find his identity in an increasingly complex society.

In 1945, Mathews published a book that critics referred to as an Osage version of Thoreau's *Walden*. In *Talking to the Moon: Wildlife Adventures on the Plains and Prairies of Osage Country*, he chronicled his homecoming, the building of his cabin on a ridge overlooking the prairie, and the passing seasons spent mostly with native wildlife and his hunting dogs. Mathews' observations are complemented by Osage cultural lore, much of it gathered from the few remaining full-bloods still knowledgeable about tribal religion and traditions.

Mathews would also write a biography of pioneer oilman E. W. Marland. Yet more than anything else, his time in the blackjacks revolved around research for his ambitious and detailed labor of love, *The Osages: Children of the Middle Waters*. Published by the University of Oklahoma Press in 1961, *The Osages* covered the history of the tribe from original creation legends to settlement in what was to become Osage County, Oklahoma.

No other scholar came close to matching Mathews' thoroughness or the painstaking manner in which he traced the evolution of what was once considered the most powerful tribe in America. His timing couldn't have been better: the last full-bloods who still retained memories of Osage culture, religion, and history were aging quickly. Also, the dominance of white culture left many of the old Osages in doubt of the veracity of the old ways and mores, and they had put away their Osageness, feeling that traditional lifestyles held little hope for the generations yet to come.

Still, Mathews was able to coax some of the elders into helping him preserve the stories and traditions that would vanish upon their deaths. It helped that he spoke the language and shared the blood. Mathews also became a member of the tribal council and played a role in helping the tribe acculturate to their newly found wealth when oil was discovered beneath the reservation.

Oil money did much to hasten the death of the traditional Osage way of life. It also did much to dilute tribal bloodlines. With profound wealth came the inevitability of intermarriage. The Osages rapidly became a mixed-blood race, and as the full-bloods disappeared, their tribal memories vanished with them.

Mathews' respect for the last of the old-time Osages comes across in his writings, as in the epitaph he penned for Osage Chief Red Eagle, printed in *Sooner Magazine* in February 1930 upon the old chief's passing: "For ninety years Red Eagle had lived among his people. For that many years of constant changes, contacts and shifting scenes, he remained an Indian; thinking Indian thoughts and dreaming his own dreams. In his later years he seemed to be waiting for something. He lived quietly on his ranch, preferring his horse to a car until he reached his eightieth year. He had oil royalties, but desired to live in simplicity. He had seen many things, and had taken part in wars in the southern part of the state; he talked of these wars with members of the tribe. He saw brick buildings rise up among the jack-oaks, and his Nation spanned with roads; some of them sinuous black ribbons winding over sandstone ridges and limestone prairie. He watched with passivity, shiny oil derricks spring up like phantasmal fungi, from valleys, wooded hills and prairie. Yet, with him remained the spirit of his fathers. To the end he remained an Indian. Frenzied wealth seeking and confused material progress did not disturb the soul of Red Eagle."

The progeny of Red Eagle would continue to play a leadership role among the Osages for decades to come, just as John Joseph Mathews would devote most of his adult life to his people. Mathews was only an eighth Osage, but his soul was 100 percent Indian. He had the intellectual tools and personality to excel in the business world but instead chose to return home, live without running water or electricity, and seek to salvage the culture of a people rapidly disappearing from the face of the earth.

Among Mathews' many achievements was the establishment of the Osage Tribal Museum, the oldest of its kind in America and still actively engaged in cultural activities on Agency Hill in Pawhuska. But John Joseph wasn't just an academician. Inscribed in Latin on his cabin fireplace is the motto he lived by: "To Hunt, to Bathe, to Play, to Laugh, that is to Live." Mathews wasn't just a tenant on his parcel of prairie earth—he was a living part of the place, drawing sustenance from the wildfowl, the water, the grass, giving back his gift of words in an effort to protect what remained of its natural heritage.

Relatives recall that a number of prominent people came to visit Mathews during his time in the sandstone cabin. They sat by the fireplace and listened to whip-poor-wills calling on summer nights or Hereford bulls bellowing their battle cries under a sizzling sun. And when the visitors would inquire about directions to the restroom, Mathews would smile and hand them a shovel. Life in the blackjacks revolved around simplicity, a perfect refuge for a complex and visionary mind.

John Madson was a legend among those of us who were learning to write about the outdoors in the early 1970s. Brimming with Earth Day enthusiasm, we strove to infuse wildlife conservation and environmentalism into the standard blood-and-guts stories that headlined a staunchly conservative hook and bullet press. In Madson, the acknowledged master of outdoor writing at the time, we discovered a hero who could catch a fish, sight in a rifle, name the wildflowers, and, with a deft stroke of his pen, turn a sunrise over the prairie or a campfire under spreading oaks into pure poetry.

Madson grew up along Iowa's Skunk River, where he learned to love prairies and the rivers that watered them. He also had a deep appreciation for sturdy pioneer stock like his Norwegian grandparents, who had settled in the Upper Midwest. Yet as much as he admired these stern, unyielding immigrants, young Madson grew into manhood watching the last of Iowa's wilderness plowed up for fields of corn, and in many ways I believe he mourned the passing of the wild more than he admired the civilization that tamed it. This love of nature led him to Iowa State University, where he earned a bachelor's degree in wildlife biology and a master's degree in fisheries biology.

Madson's studies at Iowa State provided a solid foundation for a young man whose flair for writing dovetailed nicely into outdoor reporting for the *Des Moines Register* and a job editing the Iowa Conservation Commission's magazine, *Iowa Outdoors*. Eventually John left the conservation commission to work for Winchester-Western's conservation department. His job, as he described it, was to "promote professional game management and wildlife biology."

John attacked the task with his typewriter, producing booklets about the majority of North American game animals. I first encountered these marvelous little publications when, as a young staffer on the Oklahoma Department of Wildlife Conservation's magazine *Outdoor Oklahoma*, I sought research material for the features I was assigned to write. Stuffed in our files were John's minipaperbacks detailing the lives of animals ranging from white-tailed deer to cottontail rabbits, and when I started reading I found I couldn't stop. Rather than dry textbooks, these were living prose, and I found that I wanted to collect every one and read them over and over.

This led to even more rummaging through the files, searching for even more Madson to read. In doing so, I discovered that the man who could turn the life history of a mallard duck into classic prose also wrote prolifically for the best natural history publications of the period—*Audubon*, *Smithsonian*, and *National Geographic*. *Audubon* in the early seventies produced a stunningly beautiful magazine edited by Les Line. Line sought to tell the conservation story through inspiration rather than page upon page of persistently bleak environmental horror stories, and he did this by building a stable of contributors that included the nation's best nature writers and photographers. At the top of the list was Iowa's own John Madson.

John's magazine articles covered topics ranging from tiny Platt National Park in my home state of Oklahoma to his abiding love of unplowed prairie. Each entry was typical Madson—a tongue-in-cheek pinch of humor, lyrical sentences, down-to-earth appreciation for his subject matter, and a stylistic sense that enabled him to paint vivid word pictures without seeming grandiose. When John Madson wrote about the outdoors, his words were like a magic carpet ride. The sounds, the smells, the bite of the wind were all wrapped up in his words, and the reader knew that this was a writer who had lived and loved those things he wrote about.

Eventually Madson's work began to appear in books. *Out Home* was a collection of stories penned for magazines including *Outdoor Life*, *Sports Afield*, *Guns and Ammo*, and *Audubon* between 1961 and 1977. The twenty-one essays were classic Madson, celebrating forgotten stretches of riverbank alive with migrating ducks and geese, wicked winter storms, frozen marshes, and the winged aura of that Upper Midwest import, the ring-necked pheasant. Another collection of essays, *Stories from under the Sky*, examined wildlife from badgers to shrews and dogfish to water bugs.

The Madson book that drew national attention was John's classic *Where the Sky Began: Land of the Tallgrass Prairie*. Published in 1982 and still in print today, this work did for Madson what the desert did for writers like Joseph Wood Krutch and Edward Abbey. Finally this neglected part of America's original wild landscape had a voice, and Madson was hailed as the dean of the nation's prairie restoration movement. Following publication of *Where the Sky Began*, anyone wanting something written that had to do with grasslands had Madson on speed dial. John followed his prairie book with *Up on the River: People and Wildlife of the Upper Mississippi*, a classic Madson overview of the Upper Mississippi River and the characters that interact with it, both two- and four-legged. Eventually illness slowed his writing, but until the end John remained the voice of the prairie, inspiring a growing movement to save a significant portion of what was left of it.

Madson was particularly interested in preserving the vestiges of tallgrass prairie still to be found in his home territory, including Iowa and Illinois and along the Upper Mississippi. He and other prairie preservationists also hoped that someday a sizable chunk of the Kansas Flint Hills might be included in a national park. Therefore, when the Nature Conservancy acquired the core area for its Tallgrass Prairie Preserve at the southern end of the Flint Hills in Oklahoma's Osage County, John arrived to take a look.

John loved the fact that pilots flying over sparsely populated northern Osage County referred to the countryside as the black hole due to a lack of night lights, an excellent indication that humanity lived elsewhere. One of his stamps of approval for pure prairie was that it occupied a blank spot on the map, and in this case the Nature Conservancy's new grassland acquisition definitely qualified.

Madson wouldn't be around to see the conservancy's bison herd swell to some 3,000 animals, but I'm sure he saw the animals in his mind as he gazed out over the rolling grassland on a late winter's day soon after the conservation group made its monumental acquisition. John knew the prairie and understood the invaluable biological loss if we didn't do something to save some of it. More than anything else, he was passionate about conservation, and he fought environmental cynicism with the poetry of his words.

I'll never forget his description of the prairie-chicken as "the last fading voice of the prairie wilderness, echoing after the lost clouds of curlews and plovers, crying farewell." Or his rhapsodizing about loafing in the tall prairie grasses on a summer day: "I lie there just under the wind, the grasses harping and singing faintly, their tones rising and falling, the prairie world washing over me. There is no point in moving; with a little time, the wind will bring the world to me in a steady and varied traffic. Watching under the brim of my hat I see a dragonfly . . . darting downwind to the slough off below. Next comes a squadron of monarch butterflies on their way to some crimson patch of butterfly milkweed. A male bobolink arrives twenty feet above me, hanging on the wind and stating his territorial claims with a flow of bubbling song, and then slides off to the east. His departure reveals the red-tailed hawk that he had eclipsed—a mote that swings and drifts, too high to be hunting and too late to be migrating, and plainly soaring just for the sheer exuberant hell of it, exulting in the prairie thermals that cushion his pinions from below and the prairie sun that beats on them from above. The hawk appears to be busily occupied, but he doesn't fool me. He's just another loafer. It takes one to know one." That's pure John Madson. To read the words was to know the man.

"The wealth of the tallgrass was its undoing," Madson said, referring to the richness of the soil it had built over thousands of years—dark organic soil that sang a siren's song to farmers and their wheat, soybeans, and corn. But in the Flint Hills, where rocks litter the surface like broken tile, the grassland found a refuge. Today original tenants like buffalo graze over a steely landscape that turned back the plow, and to a large extent the buffalo's shaggy presence is due to a native grasslander who dreamed about the past and better days yet to come and gave the land he loved his voice.

The obituary spelled out what those of us who knew John had dreaded since that bleak day when he revealed his illness. "Nature writer John Madson was buried last month at Jefferson Barracks National Cemetery, on the bluffs overlooking his beloved Mississippi River. Mr. Madson died April 19, 1995, at Alton Memorial Hospital. He

Poet of the Prairie

was 71 and lived in Godfrey (Illinois)." What the obituary didn't mention was that the natural world had lost one of its best friends. Several years earlier *St. Louis Post-Dispatch* writer Tim Renken, in a review of one of John's books, said that Madson "writes about nature and the outdoors as well as anybody who ever lived." That was his proper epitaph, because no truer sentence ever found its way into print.

GONE IN NOVEMBER

November in the Osage Hills is a time of transition. If the frosts are late, warm days and mild nights may linger well into the month. But the weather can also be fickle—one year on an early November day, the temperature dropped from a high in the seventies to the low teens within a few hours. The following morning, green leaves were frozen solid. They soon fell to the ground, a demoralizing gray-green. That November there were no reds, oranges, and bright yellows to accent the mists that hover over stream valleys on crisp mornings. Instead, the world turned from green to brown overnight.

During more moderate Novembers, butterflies continue to search for the last of the autumn flowers and dragonflies dance over pools renewed by October rains. Unfortunately mosquitoes linger as well, along with the ticks that have been the bane of mammals large and small throughout the summer.

Light frosts rarely kill late autumn asters, and day-flying insects continue to feast. But the most truthful voice of the season can be heard in the poignancy of field cricket chirping. The insect keys its cadence to temperature—rising or falling rates correspond to the thermometer. Slow, well-spaced calls on a chilly night seem edged with particular sadness due to the inescapable finality of the message. The season of sunlight, of flowers, trilling insects, and birdsong, is grinding to a halt. Impending change can also be witnessed in the increased angle of sunlight, a hard-edged autumn light that adds drama to November landscapes. A starkly defined autumn sunset seems a solar system away from the diffused light of summer, a flat light ripe with moisture, that can make distant horizons seem slightly out of focus in mid-June.

The moon of November arrives amid restlessness. Hunters fidget from an ancestral urge to be afield, their edginess attuned to a seasonal clock that summons whitetail bucks out of the oaks. Pushing caution aside, the deer roam the prairie searching for hormonally charged scent, stopping periodically to polish headgear armament on some stunted redcedar, leaving behind glandular evidence of their passing. These scent posts and urine scrapes are the whitetail equivalent of billboards, proclaiming to rivals that the does of surrounding oak mottes and meadows must be recognized as the property of the messenger. Disputed messages may lead to physical confrontation, where older and wiser heads generally prevail.

This period of hormonal dominance is glorious but short. A buck in his prime may dominate mating jousts for a few years, but in time antlers grow smaller, teeth succumb to wear, body mass shrinks, and a former monarch of the prairies may find himself skulking away in defeat following a fight with a younger buck. In the grand scheme of things, it's simply a matter of a healthier animal infusing vitality into the gene pool, something essential to overall good health among all living things.

I can recall frosty November nights under a full moon when trees stood like shadows pressed against a silver carpet of grass. Once, in the middle of a roadside meadow, a buck stood out, gray-brown winter coat reflecting liquid moonlight, antlers projecting the sheen of polished metal. The animal was in his prime, two hundred pounds or more, a snapshot of bloodshot passion. He was posed like a statue beneath twelve points of branching weaponry, neck swollen with a surge of testosterone. The moonlight presence of such a buck turns a frosty night into a fable, one with a tendency to linger and grow with each telling.

Then, as if released from a spell of witchery, the majestic animal slipped back into the darkness and disappeared. Mature bucks, the survivors, use darkness as their ally. But the younger bucks, especially those approaching their second birthdays, generally pay little heed to break of day and continue to sniff for doe scent, hormones totally overwhelming any caution. As a result, these are the bucks that die by the thousands on late November mornings, as they carelessly traipse into the line of fire on opening day of deer season.

At times it's almost incredible to watch, the way these young bucks pester a doe coming into estrus. Once along the Salt Fork of the Arkansas River, I watched a desperate doe seeking respite from overbearing suitors race into a farmer's front yard. It was midmorning, and she appeared exhausted by the three young bucks that clung to her every step, completely ignoring the highway traffic, the proximity of the farmhouse, and the farmer's barking dogs. The bucks were incessant in their badgering and the doe needed refuge and rest, and in her despair she sought out the proximity of that which she should have feared the most. In a few days deer season would begin, and the young bucks' ardor would be converted into venison. The doe would mate with the emperor of the moonlight shadows, the buck that had managed to escape death during his own reckless youth and developed wisdom along the way.

Bobcat Canyon, on the western edge of the southern Flint Hills in Osage County, is a depression cut by a spring with a perennial flow. Rangeland surrounding the canyon is undulating limestone prairie, excellent cattle-ranching country, and good wildlife habitat as well. When my sister lived a few miles from Bobcat Canyon, we rode there almost every weekend. We'd find newborn whitetail fawns hidden in the grass, and once a female badger defended her young by charging our horses, snarling her anger and appearing at least ten times larger than her fifteen or so pounds. Another time a prairie falcon came jetting out of the horizon, eye high, and almost took my hat off. Always, it seemed, there were coyotes and bobcats, hawks and owls, and winter eagles.

When my sister rode there with her girlfriends, they'd often race to the lone cottonwood marking the spring, arriving just in time to save the imaginary outlaw with the heart of gold (or the sultry looks of Elvis Presley) about to be hanged from a stout branch by cold-hearted vigilantes. Now these were women in their mid-thirties with jobs and children, living paycheck to paycheck, but given good horses and the seclusion of a magical place, their minds were prone to shed twenty years or more at the sound of shod hooves striking flinty rock.

At times I liked to walk to the canyon, past where a rancher, survivor of multiple marriages, liked to use her riding lawn mower as an excuse for an allover tan. Next was a small tract of agricultural land where upland sandpipers gathered to sift for leftover grain during their autumn migration. Then into the big pasture cut in half by Bobcat Canyon. There among the stark limestone ledges awaited snakes, birds, and solitude.

One Saturday in late November, I'd stopped to rest where the limestone outcropped near the mouth of the canyon, on the northeast side. This was a steep flank, dropping almost vertically to a ribbon of timber growing along a narrow prairie stream. It was a beautiful morning, temperature in the fifties, high thin clouds scattering the pallid light. It was also the first morning of deer season, the main season allowing high-powered firearms, a fact that I'd forgotten at the time.

Generally on the first morning of gun season, you can hear the rifles crackling like fireworks. The popping begins at first light, when the deer start to move, and recedes as the sun climbs higher. Therefore, early in the morning on the first day of rifle season, a lot of deer learn about rifles and hunting the hard way.

On this opening morning, there weren't any firearms breaking the silence of Bobcat Canyon. But there was a slight movement on the slope below where I sat. When I managed to focus on the spot where I thought I'd seen the grass move, I was startled to see a whitetail buck crawling slowly up to the summit. He was pressed against the earth as tightly as he could get and occasionally glanced back at the timbered valley below.

I scanned the trees along the stream and immediately saw why the buck was stretched out on his belly, edging up the steep incline. Two hunters, both wearing the blaze orange hats and vests required during gun season, were walking on either side of the timber, hoping to flush a deer out of one of the many thickets bordering the stream. Evidently the belly-crawling buck, edging along as stealthily as possible only some twenty-five yards away from my feet, had smelled or seen them coming and decided that going straight uphill was his best opportunity for escape.

I could understand the animal's desire to top the crest and become lost in the gullies and ravines of the surrounding prairie, where hunters would be scarce. But I expected him to use his excellent speed and stamina to make a break for it. This patient, careful retreat by making himself invisible against the earth was something I'd never seen from a deer. The buck was so preoccupied with the hunters that he failed to sense that I was sitting on the rock ledge nearby. I remained quiet, hoping to see what he would do.

When the buck reached the edge of the slope, he continued to crawl, still glancing back to gauge the location of the hunters. Rather than jumping to his feet, he edged forward on his belly until he reached a sumac patch about six feet tall and dense enough to conceal a cautious deer. At this point he eased into the thick cover and disappeared.

The buck was a magnificent animal, antlers widespread and toting a solid ten points. It was obvious why the two men, edging up on the thickets a hundred yards below, wanted his silhouette in their rifle scopes' crosshairs. Ever since that day I've wondered if maybe the buck had been wounded, but I never saw blood or heard the sound of rifle fire, and I'd been up since dawn. More and more I think the deer wanted to sneak up the canyon and retreat to the prairie beyond, found his pathway blocked by hunters, and decided to take a stealthy shortcut. In my mind that buck lived a long life in the vicinity of Bobcat Canyon, fathering a number of fawns and endowing them with the caution and ability to improvise that would ensure long lives of their own.

Near where Charley Creek flows into the Arkansas River along the Kansas-Oklahoma border, a large bur oak tree overshadows other bur oaks, the trees widely spaced along the edge of a farm field that was once tallgrass prairie. The oak appears to rival the size of state-record trees. But since few tree measurers wander the edge of these woods, this particular giant has remained just another big tree among many, king of the oaks in a landscape where for centuries grass dominated and fire was the master gardener.

The big oak crept out into the grassland from among trees growing along the Arkansas—a big river here, a quarter mile across the main channel in places. As one of the region's major rivers, the Arkansas has, over time, become ecologically dominant enough to acquire a forest of its own, including bur oaks poised to invade bordering grasslands.

The big bur oak of Charley Creek most likely sprouted from an acorn back when only a few Frenchmen knew of this well-watered country where once Osage and Pawnee Indians battled for hunting rights. Over time, the trees would remain regally indifferent as the land changed from a wilderness providing for a few thousand hunting and foraging Native Americans to farms, ranches, and oil fields.

Over centuries, the oak watched as Anglo immigrants replaced Paw-nee, Wichita, and Osage. The newcomers, an ambitious, restless peo-ple, staked their claim to the land with barbed wire fences and steel plows, utilizing the tools of agricultural dominion to convert most of the flatland bordering the bur oaks' parklike blend of trees and grass into tillable acreage. When they were done, these terraces above the Arkansas River where big bluestem grass once grew seven to ten feet tall were transformed into orderly rows of wheat and corn.

Unfortunately, the big tree couldn't give voice to the history that transpired beyond its boughs. However, the language of conservation biology proclaimed that the oak was certifiably old and had witnessed much. While the aged tree shared the fencerow with elms from Rus-sia, hedge apples from shelterbelt plantings, and eastern redcedars spread from bird droppings, it was evident to those who understood the nature of bur oaks that the tree had taken root in open native prai-rie. The massive trunk rose only a few feet before spreading lateral branches thicker than the main trunks of some of the bordering oaks, limbs that sank under their own immense weight as they reached out farther than the parent tree stood tall.

The immense volume of tough, heavy wood contained within the tree became most obvious in winter, when the crooked limbs were etched in silhouette against a waning sun. Even the slimmest branch seemed massive in the magic of midwinter twilight, due to a thickness of the outer bark.

The insulating properties of bur oak bark were instrumental in allowing the species to invade grassland edges where periodic fires were a matter of fact. This fire-resistant native survived where seed-lings of other oak species could not. In time, the invaders grew big enough to produce a crop of acorns to be transported even farther out into the grass with the help of willing accomplices. Most of the acorns would be retrieved as needed by the squirrels that buried them. But if even one was overlooked and managed to germinate, put down roots, and grow, then the advancing bur oak army gained another twenty yards in its battle to establish a foothold on the prairie.

Bur oaks battle for survival by putting down roots that may pen-etrate four and a half feet deep the first year. Photosynthesis takes place in lobed leaves that can be twelve inches long. The wood is some of the densest in America, tough enough to resist straight-line winds that reach ninety miles an hour or tornadoes that literally twist off the trunks of lesser oaks. Over time, the big trees take on the aura of a fortress, with their ability to withstand the ravages of wind and fire. Spreading limbs grow close enough to the ground for a man to reach up and touch, limbs as large in diameter as the mast of an old time man-o'-war bristling with British cannons.

No wonder that bur oaks served as shade for important frontier gatherings. In 1825, on the upper Neosho River, a party of American dignitaries met with representatives of the Osage Nation. They gathered beneath the boughs of a great bur oak to discuss a treaty that would allow wagons safe passage through Osage territory, along what would come to be known as the Santa Fe Trail. The Osages agreed to this adventure in international commerce and received eight hundred dollars. The Americans achieved a lucrative flow of goods to new markets and a gateway to territorial expansion that eventually included the states of New Mexico, Arizona, and California.

According to the Kansas Historical Society, the main trunk of the oak shading the gathering stood around 70 feet high and boasted a circumference of 16 feet. It grew with similar oaks along a beautiful tallgrass prairie stream in a grove including the last big timber to be seen along the trail, other than scattered cottonwoods, until travelers reached the Rocky Mountains.

The historic bur oak of Council Grove, Kansas, no longer stands. Eventually a wild prairie wind took it down. However, you can still find similar bur oaks along what were once pristine prairie streams, old-timers reaching 84 feet tall with circumferences of 18 feet or more. One bur oak, still growing along the Red River dividing Texas and Oklahoma, spreads its massive limbs some 326 feet over rich bottomland soil.

Bur oak limbs can be awe-inspiring, especially the ones that spread a few feet above the ground, big as bridge girders. Yet it's the acorns that generally cause the uninitiated to exclaim about the tree's uniqueness. Bur oak acorns are the biggest of the oak tribe, with those benefiting from long growing seasons measuring as much as two inches in diameter overall. Adding to their uniqueness is the tough acorn cup ringed with fringelike bristles, each artfully curled.

Acorns of the white oak tribe mature in a single growing season and lack the amount of tannin associated with the red oak group. Thus they're sweeter, relished by wildlife, and have long served as a staple food source for birds, animals, and early humans. One can imagine a squirrel's anticipation as a bumper crop of bur oak acorns, big as cherry tomatoes, prepares to ripen. Bur oaks only occasionally flood the wildlife market with a massive acorn crop, relying instead on a periodic approach known as masting. Every few years the parent tree expends enough resources to overwhelm its surroundings with big, fat sweet acorns. Hopefully these periodic bumper crops meet the insatiable demands of bur oak diners with a few left over—even just a handful of acorns, buried by squirrels and never recovered, adds new trees to the next generation.

Researchers studying bur oaks in the Flint Hills near Manhattan, Kansas, found that fox squirrels traveled an average of 59 feet from the parent tree before caching their prized food source. During the same study, researchers also found acorns that had been moved as far as 169 feet. Obviously the bur oaks' invasion of the grassland was slow and steady, along with an occasional leap of faith. Back when black bears roamed the prairies, it was said that a hungry bruin would rip an entire limb from a tree to get at the acorns. White travelers among the Osages in the nineteenth century mentioned that in lean times, a gruel of white oak acorns sated tribal hunger.

Today it's increasingly difficult to get a clear picture of how bur oaks successfully managed to invade the prairie's broad sea of native grass. Many of the old trees are still around, but fire suppression and agriculture have changed the nature of the landscape, and the oak openings of old are now tangled up in an untidy jungle of woody growth, much of it alien to that particular place. Before the cow and the plow, these vanguard oak groves featured trees widely spaced and separated by native tallgrass. It's not difficult to imagine why white settlers oftentimes selected these oak groves for homesites, and how the trees themselves were cut to build pioneer prairie homes.

But in the Flint Hills of Kansas and northern Oklahoma, cattle grazing proved more suited to the landscape than row crops, and much of the native plant life stayed in place. The majority of that plant life consisted of native grasses managed in the same manner utilized by the original inhabitants—periodic application of fire. Therefore, along Flint Hills streams, you can still find bur oaks dominating the headwaters, still dropping bountiful crops of big acorns every three years or so, still advancing deeper into the grass with the aid of industrious squirrels.

Few natural scenes are more serene than bur oak groves growing at the head of a Flint Hills stream valley, dark green leaves a foot long or more, grass chest high in places and sporting pale blue stems. The streams, if blessed by rain, will be clear and bouncing over gray limestone ledges. And in late summer you'll find, dangling like Christmas ornaments, the fringed cups of giant acorns clinging to sturdy branches.

Soon the fox squirrels will arrive to assist with the rugged, timeless march—twenty feet here, fifty feet there, seeds spread into the vastness with slim hope of survival. But in time one will germinate, grow quickly, and depend upon its thick bark to resist a fast-burning prairie fire. In a few hundred years it will change the landscape, but not by much.

That's because they evolved together, these grasslands and the massive trees that creep inland along meandering streams. The oaks provide mixed company that the tallgrass is willing to accommodate, but only in small doses. After that the grandiosity is up to the oaks ... but only if they survive the lightning strikes that set the grass to burning. It's tough to be a tree in a sea of grass, but bur oaks have figured out the secret. Grow a bountiful crop of acorns. Be patient. And leave the rest up to your bark.

November ended with several days of nearly constant rain, cold winds, and temperatures in the thirties. It was another chilly event provided by an El Niño–inspired weather system that brought record rainfall to the southern edge of the Flint Hills. The storm dropped some five inches of moisture that fortunately remained liquid, considering the calamity befalling the rest of the region. Farther west the temperature dipped below 32 degrees, and ice accumulations ripped the limbs from trees and tore down utility lines, leaving hundreds of thousands without electricity.

During the rain, my young Lab Cody and I mostly drove back roads looking for wildlife. Driving rural roads during inclement weather allows for a glimpse into a world that most people pass by in a hurry. On the prairie, it's a landscape where cowboys still rise before dawn to truck hay and compressed feed cubes to their cattle. During winter months, feeding cows is a daily business, something that happens come rain or come shine, what cowboys do to keep their animals fat, happy, and profitable.

Therefore, if you rise early enough and get off the blacktop roads, you'll see feed trucks slowly navigating often muddy two-track trails across reddish orange pastures, the truck sirens blasting. An electronic device mounted in the feed truck has replaced cowboys on horseback and their cattle calls. A siren certainly summons livestock from the far ends of each pasture, but I miss the cowboys and their falsetto whooping. It was a comforting sound, a wail followed by the clomping of horseshoes followed by the thunder generated by several hundred head of Hereford or Angus cattle, all hustling for a spot in the chow line.

The husband of my mother's best friend died while feeding cattle. He was in his eighties and had been a cowboy all his life, had nothing else to do and knew of nothing else he wanted to do. So his employer, a rancher who owned cattle and land on a large scale and a decent man, moved him to a small outlier ranch in Kansas, where he'd be in charge of a manageable number of cattle for as long as he was able.

The old cowboy passed away early one morning when some ranch equipment slipped from its mooring and crushed him. Afterward there was some debate concerning whether he should have moved to town and faded away into senility staring out of a dusty window, like so many other men his age. I always felt that if the jack on that outbuilding hadn't slipped, he most likely would have pushed it over himself when the right time came.

Sadly, it seems that the drivers of those muddy early morning trucks represent a way of life that's going the way of cattle calls, prairie-chickens, and the ability to make a living and still remain close to the land. Someday, maybe sooner than I'd like to think, folk in these remote ranch houses will be replaced by mega-operations with the finances to do business on a scale that won't allow heritage or nostalgia to stand in the way of profit, no matter how destructively it's obtained.

Corporate agriculture doesn't have a culture or a family tree to think about. Nor does it need to deal with the desperation of constantly living on the edge of financial meltdown. Mega-ranching won't go broke if drought steals a summer's worth of grass or if cattle markets take one of their unpredictably cantankerous nosedives. Basically, big business maintains a friend at the bank, a good lawyer, and a talented accountant who can revive a balance sheet gone awry. Small cattle operations can only hope that rain comes in the spring, calves stay healthy, and the residents of the ranch house stay healthier.

Key to all of this, of course, is the grass. Here in the remaining minuscule percentage of original tallgrass prairie, this past summer had been one that makes ranchers almost giddy. By the end of the growing season, any idle grassland was almost too dense to walk through. Even pastures that held cattle through the summer remained lush as frost in November began to turn the prairie pinkish orange.

On the Nature Conservancy's Tallgrass Prairie Preserve, the concentrated buffalo herds of the breeding season were, by December, broken up into scattered bands, the bulls staying to themselves with a few fellow bulls and the cows, calves, and yearlings grazing together in small groups. Finding buffalo here in late autumn was simple: seek out one of the many burned areas, each set afire by preserve personnel in late summer to remove hundreds of acres of mature grasses and forbs in the process of becoming dormant. Buffalo were concentrated on these burned areas, and while at first it seemed that they couldn't be finding any sort of sustenance, a closer inspection revealed a slight tinge of green scattered over the dark earth. The animals were nibbling at nutritious new shoots and appeared robust and healthy because of them.

Here amid the largest protected swath of America's remaining prairieland, grassland ecologists with the Nature Conservancy were reverting to management methods used in pre-Columbus America. Our prairies have long been manicured to attract and propagate large mammals, and fire was the tool that Native Americans used to accomplish this task. Today the curious can drive through the prairie preserve and see the results of fire management. Grazing microclimates are manufactured with a match to provide for the health of native plants plus the prosperity of nearly 3,000 bison. By manipulating both plant diversity and the length of growing seasons, grassland scientists are able to keep the herd healthy without supplying hay or commercial feed or planting supplemental crops like winter wheat. The animals manage just as their ancestors did, with renewed assistance from the prairie's new landlords, people wise enough to learn from those who came before and who knew the land intimately.

It's a rare day in the southern Flint Hills when a December drive down a county road fails to reveal bald eagles. At this time of the year you'll see all ages, both mature birds with glistening white heads and tails or brown and white streaked juveniles. Several times in early December I've encountered mature pairs feeding on roadkill, and often the repast was armadillo or, as local folk not so fondly call the creatures, rat on the half shell or canned rat.

Armadillos have moved up north from Texas as average annual temperatures have warmed. However, their arrival has not been a welcome

On the Wings of Eagles

one. Lawns and gardens tend to get turned upside down when the creatures arrive for an overnight session of grub digging, an invasion that many homeowners detest. Therefore, a splattered armadillo carcass at the edge of the road can be a welcome sight to both winged and wingless, and this particular autumn seemed to produce a great number of mashed canned rat as well as massive birds with a taste for the contents.

For two days in a row, mature eagles proved reluctant to remove themselves from a well-ripened flattened armadillo. And when they did leave, the big birds only flew as far away as a roadside fence when I approached. Each time a gathering of crows conspired to invade the dinner table so recently abandoned, a maneuver that inflamed the eagles' ire.

One day, on a high prairie plateau far removed from much of anything other than the occasional cowboy, a drive down a narrow dirt road revealed a dead coyote in a ditch and a pair of very large birds making the most of protein no longer able to bite back. I slowed down, and one of what I thought were juvenile bald eagles took wing and began to circle. The other, though, was reluctant to leave so much meat. When it finally did fly, the bird managed to cover only a few feet before landing atop a utility pole and glaring down at the motorized intruder. I stopped, reached for my camera, and realized that the pair of birds feeding on the coyote were actually golden eagles, among the most beautiful and regal animals to soar across prairie skies.

The huge bird grew nervous after a minute or so, and although still reluctant to leave the coyote carcass, it thought better of continuing such a close encounter. The chocolate brown raptor launched into low flight over the prairie, then suddenly stopped, set its wings, and dropped down to grapple with something else that suddenly aroused its wrath.

The airborne eagle's target turned out to be a mature bald eagle, sitting on a pond dam less than a quarter mile from the roadside feast. Apparently the cranky young golden eagle wanted this white-headed competitor to understand that the fresh carcass still wore a golden eagle brand, rather than being an open invitation to anything as lowly as bald eagles. A sweep of my binoculars revealed another mature bald eagle at the far end of the pond dam, and as I eased away the sullen, misty sky swirled with powerful wings as several pairs of eagles converged to debate the fate of the remaining roadkill.

Maybe a mile in the background were the spinning blades of wind turbines, violating what once had been a pristine view of the limestone breaks overlooking Salt Creek. The Osage tribe fought to block the project, but the courts found in favor of the Italian company building the wind farm, and construction went ahead with a crew from Denver, Colorado.

Public relations efforts by the wind industry promise jobs for local communities, but in this case the only money changing hands was between the landowner leasing his property and the investors. Local schools didn't benefit due to generous tax breaks, and energy consumers didn't catch a rate break either, since the power generated was destined to go elsewhere. Instead, thousands of acres of scenic Flint Hills tallgrass prairie were reduced to garish towers, flashing lights, and huge windmill blades revolving fast enough to pulverize eagles and demolish songbirds and bats by the thousands. Wind power is advertised as being environmentally friendly, but this seems a hollow claim when the rarest of places and the rare life forms clinging to existence here are mutilated beyond recognition and the sanctity of their homes utterly destroyed.

West of Pawhuska and far out on the prairie there's a little cemetery that, according to folklore, is occupied by a pair of cowboys who fought over a woman. Legend has it that, following an exchange of gunfire, both died and were buried where they fell. Late one winter afternoon the waning sun shed a low layer of clouds, and in the brightness I noticed several large birds soaring over the graves. The sharp edge of sunlight described a telltale silhouette of circling bald eagles. Four were on the wing, and the December sun reflected off the brilliant white feathers that revealed their maturity.

Rather than hunting, these birds were making tight, low, sometimes almost lazy circles, dipping and diving, their flight seemingly synchronized. When two of the birds dropped in unison as if they'd been shot and clasped talons as they fell, I realized that mating bonds were in the process of being established. Soon the paired raptors would retreat to one of several massive stacks of treetop sticks scattered across the countryside. There, despite snow, sleet, hail, and wind with a reputation for ripping limbs from trees, the birds would depend upon each other to brood eggs and hunt and eventually, in a tall cottonwood either out in some prairie pasture or maybe in timber bordering the banks of a prairie river, they'd defy such cruel odds and fledge young.

On the Wings of Eagles

By the time patches of pale white anemones dotted surrounding spring grasslands, these resident eagles would be deep into the process of combing the countryside for that coot, rabbit, songbird, or squirrel vital to a successful nesting cycle. These birds, going about their daily business, remain a sight that has stirred emotions over centuries. For me at least, if there's a wild signature that truly represents these United States, it's an eagle on the wing, pressed against a blue sky dappled with puffy white clouds. Add a backdrop of rolling prairie grassland, still functioning in a timeless and natural fashion, and I'm convinced that the last best place on earth resides directly under my feet. It's a landscape worth saving simply because of the biological wealth that these grasslands represent—there is nothing quite like these green hills anywhere else on the planet.

When William L. Lovely joined several thousand migrant Cherokee homesteading along the banks of the White and Arkansas Rivers in what is now the state of Arkansas, the newly appointed agent complained about the wasteful habits of white hunters who'd followed the Indians west. Lovely told his supervisors back in Washington, D.C., that the whites were destroying the resources the Cherokee needed to survive. They were killing buffalo in great numbers just for the tallow and leaving the carcasses to rot. He complained that the spoiled meat alone could have sustained the Indians, adding that bears in the region were also slaughtered with the meat and hides left behind, as the white hunters wanted only the oil the animals yielded.

Within a few years, the Cherokee were petitioning for more hunting land farther west, as the game in the area had been depleted. Land along the Arkansas and White Rivers had been Osage hunting territory, yielded to the Cherokee newcomers via treaty. Now the Cherokee wanted hunting rights farther up the Arkansas, the Verdigris, and Neosho Rivers in what is now Oklahoma. They also wanted the Osages pushed farther north and west, away from this fecund region.

By this time, the Osages were resolved to fight the Cherokee due to the latter's incursions into country the Osages claimed as their own.

Therefore in 1824, in an effort to keep the peace, the army constructed Fort Gibson where the Neosho and Verdigris Rivers joined the Arkansas. The place was known throughout the frontier as Three Forks, due to the proximity of the rivers. Three Forks soon became the commercial capital of the new West, with several companies operating trading posts where the rivers merged.

There was still wild game in the Osage country in 1824, evidenced in orders given to soldiers stationed at Fort Gibson. If they wanted meat in their diet, they were to kill a buffalo. At the same time, traders operating out of Three Forks, where they mainly dealt with Osage trappers and hunters, were shipping numerous hides down the Arkansas to the Mississippi River and then to New Orleans.

In his book *Pioneer Days in the Early Southwest*, historian Grant Foreman wrote that in April 1824, employees of Auguste Chouteau, a successful Three Forks trader, loaded a barge bound downriver. When they finished, the boat held 38,757 pounds of furs and skins. On board were some 300 female bear skins, 160 skins taken from bear cubs, 387 beaver pelts, 67 otter pelts, 720 cat hides including bobcats and cougars, 95 fox pelts, and 364 bales of deer hides. Separate from the deerskins Chouteau had traded for were 726 hides shipped to market by another French trader, Pierre Menard.

Other traders in the area shipped similar numbers of furs and hides to market, keeping the Osages busy due to the tribe's desire for arms, powder, and lead to defend their territory from the Cherokee and other tribes moving west to escape white settlers overrunning their original homelands east of the Mississippi. One notable absence from Chouteau's shipment was buffalo hides. The influx of subsistence hunters and their desire for buffalo meat and robes had pushed these animals farther west at a pace dictated by the mushrooming numbers of hunters and settlers flowing into the region.

In 1832, writer Washington Irving kept a journal of his adventures while exploring unmapped territory in what is now the state of Oklahoma. Later he wrote a book about his travels called *A Tour on the Prairies*, and in it he describes meeting with several Osage hunters near modern Oklahoma City. The Indians told Irving's group that their hunger for buffalo meat would soon be sated when they arrived at the "prairies on the banks of the Grand Canadian," where they'd find plenty of game. That same year Commissioner of Indian Settlement Henry Ellsworth complained that "a few years since, buffalo were seen around the garrison of Fort Gibson—now they never approach within 100 miles of it, and we found them 170 miles distant" while traveling west with Irving's exploratory party.

Two years later, when artist George Catlin joined an expedition of U.S. Army Dragoons headed west from Fort Gibson to make contact with the Plains Indians, the soldiers didn't discover bison in quantity until they reached a point along the Canadian River where Norman, Oklahoma, stands today, near the junction of modern interstate highways I-40 and I-35. In his book *Letters and Notes on the Manners, Customs, and Conditions of North American Indians*, Catlin reported that he and the dragoons were "snugly encamped on a beautiful plain, and in the midst of countless numbers of buffaloes; and halting a few days to recruit our horses and men, and dry meat to last us the remainder of our journey."

The artist noted that "the plains around this, for many miles, seem actually speckled in distance, and in every direction, with herds of grazing buffaloes." Catlin said that "the men have dispersed in little squads in all directions, and are dealing death to these poor creatures to a most cruel and wanton extent, merely for the pleasure of *destroying*, generally without stopping to cut out the meat. During yesterday and this day, several hundreds have undoubtedly been killed, and not so much as the flesh of half a dozen used. Such immense swarms of them are spread over this tract of country; and so divided and terrified have they become, finding their enemies in all directions where they run, that the poor beasts seem completely bewildered—running here and there, and as often as otherwise, come singly advancing to the horsemen, as if to join them for their company, and are easily shot down."

Buffalo managed to survive on the southern plains until the 1870s, when a new market for hides to be used as industrial machine belts sealed their fate. By the turn of the twentieth century there were, essentially, no deer, otters, cougars, bears, or buffalo in the region. Yet less than a century before, entrepreneurs enjoyed booming businesses built upon shipping their hides, furs, tallow, and oil downriver by the ton. Relocated Indian tribes quickly killed for their own use any wildlife that escaped commercial exploitation. And wherever the Indians went, restless whites, blacks, and immigrants of all races followed.

It was an unbelievable onslaught, humanity against nature, and today it's hard to imagine that just decades before all this extinction,

Pastures of Plenty

natural historians exploring in the Osage homeland wrote of Carolina parakeets, ivory-billed woodpeckers, and passenger pigeons in flocks that shaded out the sun. These three species were extinct in the region by the turn of the twentieth century.

It's difficult not to daydream about the journeys of explorers like George Catlin and Washington Irving, especially while sitting alone on the prairie on a June day. The landscape seems vibrant with so much green potential that it begs for the return of creatures once an integral part of its natural order. Destroying, for profit, the wildlife once common here seems an act of treason against what so many hold sacred. Yet contemporary religious doctrine basically remains indifferent—or even approving—when life on this planet succumbs to shortsightedness and greed.

It's not easy for those of us who love wildlife and wild landscapes to watch a native species, a part of these prairies for tens of thousand of years, decline and then disappear within the meager time frame of a lifetime. As a child, I helped my father train pointers and setters for quail hunting throughout the mixed oak woodland and tallgrass prairie surrounding our home. People from the region made appointments to hunt with my dad, due to the numbers of quail we had access to and the quality of his dogs. Half a century later, high-quality quail hunting in Oklahoma is mostly a memory. Greater prairie-chickens were also once common on the prairies around my childhood home and a popular game bird. Now they're protected, and the last healthy booming ground gathering I saw was on the Nature Conservancy's Tallgrass Prairie Preserve, just south of the Kansas state line.

Land use changes have affected upland game hunting here on the southern edge of the Flint Hills, a sport that was, in the 1950s, among the region's favorite outdoor activities. Grassland birds have declined because the quality of native grassland has declined. We lament that so little of the original prairie remains unplowed, while even the remaining percentage isn't by any means pristine. Much of it has been degraded by overgrazing, the invasion of noxious alien plants, the continued encroachment of woody vegetation, and herbicide spraying to kill "weeds." Sadly, these so-called weeds oftentimes are native broadleaved plants that provide food and shelter for grassland birds on the cusp of disappearing from the planet.

Domestic livestock, the alleged beneficiary of herbicide application, would be better served by grasslands more in balance with the original, because the forbs and legumes now killed by chemicals can be high in protein and also return vital nutrients to the soil, allowing for more vigorous grasses. Buffalo, the Osages' wild cattle, utilize the grassland differently from cattle breeds imported from Europe. As a result, the buffalo's return to the Nature Conservancy's Tallgrass Prairie Preserve has resulted in a shabbier grassland yet a healthier one, in that more leafy plants are both present and protected, allowing for greater biological diversity.

Restoring some of the original order to the preserve has been a boon to creatures ranging from butterflies to all those drab little brown birds that hide in the high grasses. At first, ranchers in the region scoffed at the transformation and alluded to the "ruination" of what was once a great ranch. But now, following decades of experimentation and scientific study, grassland researchers working at the preserve are discovering ways to utilize fire to extend grazing seasons and thus use less supplemental feed. They're sharing their newfound knowledge with the ranchers, who stand to make more money with less expense just by letting the landscape be what it was meant to be and occasionally applying a match.

Today, the majority of beef cattle in America graze in regions that were formerly more fit for a squirrel than an Angus or Hereford. Chemically and mechanically manipulated "tame" pasture fits the corporate agricultural blueprint much better than native pastures prone to the vagaries of whimsical weather patterns. It's more convenient to raise animals for food in the manner we currently raise hogs and chickens, rigidly contained and environmentally controlled. Still, many of us are nagged by the question, is it the morally right thing to do?

An alternative presents itself in the tallgrass country, where you can still see calves born and grow fat on grasses native to this place for tens of thousands of years. They roam pastures containing thousands of acres between fences and flourish in the sun, wind, and rain. An animal raised in such a manner certainly seems healthier and more nourishing than one raised in a crate and fed antibiotics to keep it alive in its deplorable confinement.

Here, on what remains of our native grasslands, we have cattle and buffalo raised to become a physical part of a healthy landscape as they take their nourishment from the earth beneath their feet. Meat produced on wild grass may not be as profitable as hamburger grown on tame pasture, but common sense tells us it must be more wholesome for both body and spirit.

If native grassland is to survive, it will most likely take new generations of friends, especially friends willing to help with and work toward providing the resources required to protect land from commercial greed. Scientists are just beginning to understand the intricacies of ecological interaction hidden away in all this grass. Their work begs the question, what greater sin can we levy against the planet of our birthright than to destroy something, lay waste to it, before we're even able to know, name, and understand all its working parts?

It's easy to agonize over the fate of what many have called America's defining landscape. But such dark thoughts disappear when thousands of bison on the prairie preserve rise from their afternoon ruminating and move in unison to where they've chosen to graze in the evening. The melodic voices of the prairie, those of meadowlark, dickcissel, and grasshopper sparrow, provide a marching song while evening colors cling to lingering clouds. Orange calves trot beside chocolate brown cows, and you begin to realize that this is a scene occurring on a wild landscape that hasn't been witnessed in this region for some two centuries—not in such numbers and not on such an extent of native grass.

On a rocky seat at the edge of the tallgrass, we get an opportunity to time travel, to be part of an American legend. Here, where many of the old natural processes once again prosper, is an opportunity to touch, to feel, to see, to smell, and most of all to protect the real wild earth of our origins.

Sycamore Creek rises from a series of springs a few miles east of the Osage village of Grayhorse. Several forks join to flow southwest to the Arkansas River, draining rolling prairie and then dense post oak–blackjack oak forest near the border with the river. It's a clear, clean little stream, flowing a dozen feet wide on average over limestone and sandstone bedrock and cobble.

Judging from the mortar holes ground into slab rock and the lithic scatter left over from flint knapping around the headwater springs, the area must have earned a four-star rating from campers long ago, people who left prehistoric villages along nearby Hominy Creek and the Arkansas River to hunt buffalo on the high prairie to the northwest. Mixed hardwood forests bordering the streams provided walnuts, acorns, hickory nuts, and pecans to grind in the smooth holes worn into bedrock. The water was sweet and good, the campsites shaded. These temporary hunting camps were well used, judging from the depth of the grinding holes and the amount of debris left from the fashioning of stone tools and projectile points.

When the Osage Indians sold their reservation in Kansas in 1870 and relocated south across the state line in what is now Osage County, one branch of the tribe settled a few miles west of the Sycamore Creek headwaters, establishing a village they called Grayhorse. A few years later, Catholic missionaries built a school for Indian boys along Hominy Creek, a few miles northeast of the Sycamore Creek springs. When the reservation was dissolved in 1907 upon Oklahoma statehood, the springs were included in what is now Bluestem Ranch, owned over the next hundred years by the daughter of one of the region's pioneer cowboys, by descendants of the locally famous Drummond ranching family, and by a billionaire from Atlanta who made a fortune in the cable news industry.

Seasonal cattle grazing on native grass range was until recently a pastoral, mostly environmentally benign pursuit. However, a harsher, more brutal industry invaded the area early in the twentieth century when vast petroleum reserves were discovered in Osage County. By midcentury a small community serving the Texas (Texaco) Company's Naval Reserve oil field consisted of maybe fifty families, a gas station, a grocery store, two churches, and an office building. Owned by the Texas Company and built on land leased from local ranchers, the houses, barely livable by modern standards and rented to employees for around fifteen dollars a month, were scattered across the prairie.

Ranchers in Osage County owned the grass but not the oil or any other subsurface minerals. Following statehood, the Osages managed to retain the mineral rights to their former reservation. As a result, oil companies including Texaco, Phillips, and Conoco worked directly with the tribe when brokering leases, negotiating drilling rights, and paying royalties. Surface landowners were reimbursed for actual physical damages, but other than that they were basically ignored by the petroleum industry.

The region around the headwaters of Sycamore Creek had a rough edge to it when my family moved there in 1947. My father found a job with the Texas Company when he returned home from Germany after World War II. I was three months old when we moved to the Naval Reserve oil camp, arriving to find my family had been provided with a three-room wood frame house with a tin roof, no insulation, no electricity, and no running water. My first bath in that house was in a washtub filled with water carried uphill in buckets by my older brother, each bucket provided by the spring flowing clear and cold some fifty yards below the house. Over the months that followed, my dad managed to add an extra room by enclosing a porch, wire the house for electricity, and lay enough pipe to provide running water in the kitchen, eliminating what my brother recalled as the seemingly endless trips to the spring for water, each bucketful hauled in a little red wagon that kids at the time coveted as much as they do video games today.

The spring yielded good water, a cool blessing from the damp dark earth that welled up in the shade of a black willow tree. Total strangers arrived at our house, jugs in hand, inquiring if they could "fetch a little water from that nice spring." They liked the water, they told my parents, because it was allegedly a health tonic. Neighbors said people had been making pilgrimages to the spring for years, filling their jugs and then pausing to gossip with elder members of the Edwards family, the original tenants dating back to the middle 1930s.

The Edwards clan raised ten children along the headwaters of Sycamore Creek. Mr. Edwards worked in the oil field but, like others of his generation, kept his family fed by adding a chicken house, milk barn, pigpen, half-acre garden plot, and a small fenced lot for a calf to be fattened for slaughter. There were native trees and shrubs that sufficed for restrooms, a pool in the creek for bathing. Our family upgraded to an outhouse that offered little comfort on freezing winter nights. For many years, it was our most modern addition next to running water, constructed squarely and securely over a gaping hole in the dense stone substrate, a wound carved wide and deep by some spare dynamite my father found in his toolshed.

The Naval Reserve oil field camp was a fixture in the area until the early 1970s, when production began to wane. People moved away, houses fell empty, stores closed. The economic pulse of the area slowed to the rhythm of cattle grazing on lush grass. Occasionally one of the few remaining oil field employees raised dust in the distance with his pickup truck, leaving a lingering signature across the landscape as he tended wells that by that time pumped more saltwater than coveted black gold.

Eventually, Texaco sold the field to a company specializing in picking the remaining particles of fiscal profit off the bones of once-prosperous oil fields. My father retired and moved to town, and as house after house fell vacant throughout the oil field, local ranchers hired bulldozers to flatten the structures and then they burned the remains. But even though the old home place was gone, my younger brother and I continued to make regular pilgrimages to the spring, to the nearby stock pond where we'd learned to swim, and to the long-

The Ghost Springs of Sycamore Creek

forgotten Indian camp where as kids we'd sit on a rock and load our cap pistols for the daily contest of cowboys and Indians.

We emulated the western actors who dominated television programs and movie theaters in the 1950s, stars including Roy Rogers, Gene Autry, the Lone Ranger, and Sky King. Most within our little urchin pack argued over playing the part of either Gene or Roy. But I always wanted to be Tonto, the Lone Ranger's stoic Native American sidekick. After all, this was Indian country, evidenced by the pink arrowheads we picked up around the springs and mast-grinding mortar holes we played among. White people, in my way of thinking, just seemed to belong somewhere else. And in fact, within the span of a couple of decades, most of them would be gone.

Once, on a golden autumn morning following a personal crisis that occurred in my mid-twenties, I made a head-clearing visit to the spring. Walking and ruminating, I ambled south from the headwaters spring to where Sycamore Creek receives the flow of several sister springs and widens into a proper creek, replete with deep holes for fishing and swimming and the beginning of a fringe woodland—big bur oaks, Shumard oaks, and bitternut hickories with smooth bark as sleek to the touch as youthful skin. Although I was despondent at the beginning of the walk, my dark thoughts were erased by the discovery of a badger digging industriously into a bordering embankment. At that exact same moment, I heard a piercing cry and looked up in time to see a bald eagle, white head and tail feathers aglow in the November sunlight.

I found a good sitting rock and reflected. Over the years, from this same maze of exposed sandstone boulders, I'd watched red foxes and curious coyotes come as close as they dared. For several years, a bobcat kept a den nearby, and although she sat quietly and watched us kids pass by more often than not, she vanished like a ghost if we carried our BB guns or, later, .22-caliber rifles, a rite of passage that diminished the innocence of our relationship to the landscape and its wildlife.

The more I thought about it, the more evident it became that the land along Sycamore Creek was rewilding as the oil field dried up. Some of the terrible scars left from pipeline breaks and saltwater spills were beginning to heal. Grass grew again where houses had been bulldozed, leaving behind only daffodils and thorny sprays of the pink and red roses that once marked gateposts made of abandoned drilling pipe. By the turn of the twenty-first century, wild turkey once again strutted along the banks of Sycamore Creek, and white-tailed deer were common. And cool springwater still welled up amid the cattails.

At the turn of the twenty-first century, even more profound change came to the prairieland bordering the Sycamore Creek springs. Ted Turner, media mogul and lover of grasslands and the bison that belong on them, bought Bluestem Ranch and began stocking it with buffalo, mostly yearling heifers that would fatten on bluestem grass before becoming commercial table fare. As a kid I'd spent countless hours roaming these hills, dreaming of the time when bison ranged across the tallgrass and Indians gathered at camps near these springs to hunt them. And then one day there they were, the shaggy beasts of western folklore, grazing over the grasslands of my youth as if they'd entered through some time portal I'd completely missed.

Ted Turner was a good steward of the land, and the prairie seemed to respond with vigor to both his methods and his grazing animal of choice. Most of the ranch's interior fencing came down, and I noticed that these young buffalo, like the larger herd at the Tallgrass Prairie Preserve only a few miles distant, were restless grazers. I'd photograph a group at one location and find them cropping grass miles away within a few hours. Loitering wasn't, it seemed, part of buffalo DNA.

Turner's tenure as landlord over the headwaters of Sycamore Creek lasted sixteen years. When the nation's largest landowner decided to sell Bluestem Ranch, I was nervous. The land remained mostly intact and ecologically viable. Somehow it had survived years of oil production and, at the end, secondary recovery methods based upon the deep injection of saltwater designed to free the last dregs of petroleum clinging to the prairie underground. I could only hope that the next owner would have the environmental conscience of a Ted Turner or the down-to-earth grassroots regard for the land of a traditional ranching family.

To be honest, I never thought about the Osages wanting some of their history restored in the form of real estate. The great wealth of the tribe waned in the second half of the twentieth century as oil production declined. But then the Osages found something just as good or maybe even better for producing income—a source of funding that doesn't pollute and in many ways seems a somewhat ironic, poetic, or even karmic reversal of fortune, considering the army of parasites that arrived to fleece the tribe out of its oil income back in the 1920s.

In recent years, Indian gaming has transformed Indian country, empowering Native Americanism financially, culturally, and philosophically. Proceeds from Osage-owned and Osage-operated casinos have been fortuitous, being invested in health, education, language, culture, and infrastructure. Therefore, when Ted Turner decided to sell his ranch in the Osage country, gaming income allowed the Osages to submit a winning bid for the property, reversing a long history of watching tribally owned lands disappear. Turner's Bluestem Ranch included 43,000 acres of native tallgrass prairie and woodland and several perennial streams—a microcosm of the old Osage homeland. As reported in the tribe's *Osage News*, Assistant Principal Chief Raymond Red Corn pointed out that when the Osage Nation Congress voted to purchase the ranch, the Osages were "extremely pleased to reverse 200 years of loss of our lands."

According to the *Osage News*, Principal Chief Geoffrey Standing Bear had written to Turner in January 2016, expressing his desire to see the property returned to tribal ownership. "These plains are part of the Osage People's original homelands," Standing Bear said. "At last we have the ability and opportunity to once again own this much land in one place." Standing Bear also told Turner how much the loss of their land had undermined the tribe's sense of place. "Until 1906 we owned nearly 1.5 million acres in one contiguous parcel of what is now Osage County," he wrote. "We now only own five percent of our original land in scattered parcels." Late in June, Standing Bear signed an application he hoped would result in fee-to-trust federal status for the 43,000-acre ranch. "Once put into trust, it cannot be sold, burdened with legal, financial obligations unless approved by the United States by trust standards," he said. "This way, I feel this land is safe from the activities of this generation and will be preserved for the next, and the next generation thereafter."

When the Osages completed the bidding process, the *Osage News* reported that Standing Bear told Ted Turner it was the tribe's intention to preserve, protect, and sustain the land as well as use it as a home for "the bison that are sacred to us." At the time Standing Bear pointed out that "we will use the lands to reconnect our children and youth to nature. We can think of no better learning environment for our children than these lands. . . . This land is perfectly centered between our traditional towns of Wa-hock-o-li (Pawhuska), Zon-zo-lin (Hominy) and Pah-su-li (Grayhorse)."

In his book *The Osages: Children of the Middle Waters*, tribal historian John Joseph Mathews pointed out that late in the nineteenth century, when the Ghost Dance revival swept through Indian country, the Osages came together at this same central location to dance for several days before losing hope and interest. An Arapaho priest named Sitting Bull brought the Ghost Dance to the Osages, promising that by dancing, praying, and leading exemplary lives, tribes throughout the region could convince a higher power to bring a great flood. The flood would do away with white people, he said, and in their place would be buffalo.

By this time, the Osages had a long history of dealing with Anglos and were skeptical. Still, the springs at the headwaters of Sycamore Creek provided a good place to gather for a few days and at least give it a try. Although the tribe may have grown tired of waiting, most of the white people actually were gone from the countryside a little over a century later, and buffalo tracks graced the mud at the edge of the springs shortly after that.

Maybe the Ghost Dance priests had it right after all, while their converts overlooked the cosmic nature of Indian time, a stereotypical lack of urgency that non-Indians sometimes take pleasure in deriding. Even so, judging from the overflow of Anglo-driven automobiles at Indian casinos and the ambitious plans of the Osages to use gaming proceeds to buy their lands back, maybe this time around it's the Indians—and the future of some fine tallgrass prairie—who will appreciate the last laugh.

Geology

Naff, John D. *Guidebook for Geologic Field Trips in North-Central Oklahoma*. Norman: University of Oklahoma Press, 1981.

Grassland Birds

Bent, Arthur Cleveland. *Life Histories of North American Shore Birds*. New York: Dover Books, 1961.

Bodsworth, Fred. *Last of the Curlews*. Berkeley, Calif.: Counterpoint Press, 2011.

Cokinos, Christopher. *Hope Is the Thing with Feathers: A Personal Chronicle of Vanished Birds*. New York: Warner Books, 2001.

Ehrlich, Paul R., David S. Dobkin, and Darryl Wheye. *Birds in Jeopardy: The Imperiled and Extinct Birds of the United States and Canada, Including Hawaii and Puerto Rico*. Palo Alto, Calif.: Stanford University Press, 1992.

Guthery, Fred S. *On Bobwhites*. College Station: Texas A&M University Press, 2006.

Hoch, Greg. *Booming from the Mists of Nowhere: The Story of the Greater Prairie-Chicken*. Iowa City: University of Iowa Press, 2015.

Johnsgard, Paul A. *Earth, Water, and Sky: A Naturalist's Stories and Sketches*. Austin: University of Texas Press, 1999.

———. *Grassland Grouse and Their Conservation*. Washington, D.C.: Smithsonian Institution Press, 2002.

———. *The Grouse of the World*. Lincoln: University of Nebraska Press, 1983.

———. *Hawks, Eagles, and Falcons of North America*. Washington, D.C.: Smithsonian Institution Press, 2004.

————. *The Plovers, Sandpipers, and Snipes of the World.* Lincoln: University of Nebraska Press, 1981.

————. *Prairie Birds: Fragile Splendor in the Great Plains.* Lawrence: University Press of Kansas, 2004.

Matthiessen, Peter. *The Wind Birds: Shorebirds of North America.* Shelburne, Vt.: Chapters Publishing, 1996.

Rising, James D. *A Guide to the Identification and Natural History of the Sparrows of the United States and Canada.* Cambridge, Mass.: Academic Press, 1996.

Sibley, David Allen. *The Sibley Guide to Birds.* New York: Alfred A. Knopf Press, 2003.

Sutton, George Miksch. *Oklahoma Birds: Their Ecology and Distribution.* Norman: University of Oklahoma Press, 1967.

Wolfe, Don. "Cowbirds." *George Miksch Sutton Avian Research Center E-zine,* 1999. http://www.suttoncenter.org/about/publications/e-zines/.

Grassland Mammals

Bailey, James A. *American Plains Bison: Rewilding an Icon.* Helena, Mont.: Sweetgrass Books, 2013.

Caire, William, Jack D. Tyler, Bryan P. Glass, and Michael A. Mares. *Mammals of Oklahoma.* Norman: University of Oklahoma Press, 1989.

Coppedge, Bryan R., and James H. Shaw. "Bison Grazing Patterns on Seasonally Burned Tallgrass Prairie." *Journal of Range Management* 51 (May 1998): 258–264. https://journals.uair.arizona.edu/index.php/jrm/article/viewFile/9309/8921.

Hornaday, William Temple. *The Extermination of the American Bison.* Washington, D.C.: Smithsonian Institution Press, 2002.

Isenberg, Andrew C. *The Destruction of the Bison.* New York: Cambridge University Press, 2001.

Johnsgard, Paul A. *Great Wildlife of the Great Plains.* Lawrence: University Press of Kansas, 2003.

Lott, Dale F. *American Bison: A Natural History.* Berkeley: University of California Press, 2002.

McHugh, Tom. *The Time of the Buffalo.* New York: Alfred A. Knopf, 1972.

Payne, Toni, Sandy Stevens, and William Caire. "Annotated Checklist of the Mammals of the Tallgrass Prairie Preserve, Osage County, Oklahoma." *Proceedings of the Oklahoma Academy of Science* 81 (2001): 41–51. http://digital. library.okstate.edu/oas/oas_pdf/v81/p41_51.pdf.

Schwartz, Charles W., and Elizabeth R. Schwartz. *The Wild Mammals of Missouri.* Columbia: University of Missouri Press, 2001.

Grassland Plants and Ecology

Allen, Matthew S., Robert G. Hamilton, Ulrich Melcher, and Michael W. Palmer. "Lessons from the Prairie: Research at the Nature Conservancy's Tallgrass

Prairie Preserve." Stillwater: Oklahoma Academy of Science, 2009. http://www.
tgp-docents.com/docent/files/Lessons-from-the-Prairie.pdf.

Bare, Janet E. *Wildflowers and Weeds of Kansas*. Lawrence: University Press of
Kansas, 2015.

Barnard, Iralee. *Field Guide to the Common Grasses of Oklahoma, Kansas, and Nebraska*.
Lawrence: University Press of Kansas, 2014.

Beitelspacher, Kindra. "Eastern Gamagrass: Queen of the Grasses." *Beef Magazine*,
March 1, 1998. http://beefmagazine.com/mag/beef_eastern_gamagrass_queen.

Christiansen, Paul, and Mark Müller. *An Illustrated Guide to Iowa Prairie Plants*. Iowa
City: University of Iowa Press, 1999.

Cobb, Boughton. *A Field Guide to the Ferns*. Boston: Houghton Mifflin, 1956.

Collins, Scott L., and Linda L. Wallace, eds. *Fire in North American Tallgrass Prairies*.
Norman: University of Oklahoma Press, 1990.

Folley, Patricia. *The Guide to Oklahoma Wildflowers*. Iowa City: University of Iowa
Press, 2007.

Gould, Frank W. *Common Texas Grasses: An Illustrated Guide*. College Station: Texas
A&M University Press, 2000.

———. *The Grasses of Texas*. College Station: Texas A&M University Press, 1975.

Great Plains Flora Association. *Flora of the Great Plains*. Lawrence: University Press
of Kansas, 1986.

Hatch, Stephan L., and Jennifer Pluhar. *Texas Range Plants*. College Station: Texas
A&M University Press, 1992.

Hitchcock, A. S. *Manual of the Grasses of the United States*. 2 vols. New York: Dover, 1971.

Kindscher, Kelly. *Edible Wild Plants of the Prairie: An Ethnobotanical Guide*. Lawrence:
University Press of Kansas, 1987.

———. *Medicinal Wild Plants of the Prairie: An Ethnobotanical Guide*. Lawrence:
University Press of Kansas, 1993.

Kirkpatrick, Zoe Merriman. *Wildflowers of the Western Plains: A Field Guide*. Austin:
University of Texas Press, 1992.

Kirt, Russell R. *Prairie Plants of the Midwest: Identification and Ecology*. Champaign,
Ill.: Stipes Publishing, 1995.

Ladd, Doug. *Tallgrass Prairie Wildflowers*. Nashville, Tenn.: Falcon Press, 1995.

Logan, William Bryant. *Dirt: The Ecstatic Skin of the Earth*. New York: W. W. Norton,
2007.

Madson, John. *Tallgrass Prairie*. Nashville, Tenn.: Falcon Press, 1993.

———. *Where the Sky Began: Land of the Tallgrass Prairie*. Iowa City: University of
Iowa Press, 2004.

Malin, James C. "An Introduction to the History of the Bluestem Pasture Region
of Kansas." Topeka: Kansas State Historical Society, 1942. https://www.kshs.
org/p/kansas-historical-quarterly-an-introduction-to-the-history-of-the-
bluestem/12894.

McCoy, Doyle. *Roadside Flowers of Oklahoma*. 2 vols. Lawton, Okla.: C and J Printing Company, 1976.

Miller, Howard A., and Samuel H. Lamb. *Oaks of North America*. Happy Camp, Calif.: Naturegraph Publishers, 1984.

Price, John T., ed. *The Tallgrass Prairie Reader*. Iowa City: University of Iowa Press, 2014.

Reichman, O. J. *Konza Prairie: A Tallgrass Natural History*. Lawrence: University Press of Kansas, 1988.

Samson, Fred B., and Fritz L. Knopf, eds. *Prairie Conservation: Preserving North America's Most Endangered Ecosystem*. Washington, D.C.: Island Press, 1996.

Shirley, Shirley. *Restoring the Tallgrass Prairie: An Illustrated Manual for Iowa and the Upper Midwest*. Iowa City: University of Iowa Press, 2002.

Smith, Annick. *Big Bluestem: Journey into the Tall Grass*. Tulsa, Okla.: Council Oak Books, 1996.

Tyrl, Ronald J., Terrence G. Bidwell, and Ronald E. Masters. *Field Guide to Oklahoma Plants: Commonly Encountered Prairie, Shrubland, and Forest Species*. Stillwater: Oklahoma State University Department of Plant and Soil Sciences, 2002.

Weaver, J. E. *Native Vegetation of Nebraska*. Lincoln: University of Nebraska Press, 1965.

———. *North American Prairie*. Chicago: Johnsen Publishing, 1954.

———. *Prairie Plants and Their Environment: A Fifty-Year Study in the Midwest*. Lincoln: University of Nebraska Press, 1968.

Whitley, James R., Barbara Bassett, Joe G. Dillard, and Rebecca A. Haefner. *Water Plants for Missouri Ponds*. Jefferson City: Missouri Department of Conservation, 1990.

Williams, Dave, and Brent Butler. *The Tallgrass Prairie Center Guide to Seed and Seedling Identification in the Upper Midwest*. Iowa City: University of Iowa Press, 2016.

History, Personalities, and Osage Indians

Catlin, George. *Letters and Notes on the Manners, Customs, and Condition of the North American Indians*. 2 vols. New York: Dover, 1973.

DeVoto, Bernard. *The Journals of Lewis and Clark*. Boston: Mariner Books, 1997.

Dodge, Richard Irving. *The Plains of the Great West*. New York: Archer House, 1959.

Foreman, Grant. *Pioneer Days in the Early Southwest*. Lincoln: University of Nebraska Press, 1994.

Francis, John, ed. *Tixier's Travels on the Osage Prairies*. Translated by Albert J. Salvan McDermott. Norman: University of Oklahoma Press, 1940.

Franks, Kenny A. *The Osage Oil Boom*. Oklahoma City: Western Heritage Books, 1989.

Hoig, Stan. *Beyond the Frontier: Exploring the Indian Country*. Norman: University of Oklahoma Press, 1998.

Irving, Washington. *A Tour on the Prairies*. Norman: University of Oklahoma Press, 1985.

La Flesche, Francis. *The Osage and the Invisible World*. Norman: University of Oklahoma Press, 1995.

Leopold, Aldo. *A Sand County Almanac*. New York: Ballantine Books, 1970.

Mathews, John Joseph. *The Osages: Children of the Middle Waters*. Norman: University of Oklahoma Press, 1995.

———. *Talking to the Moon: Wildlife Adventures on the Plains and Prairies of Osage County*. Norman: University of Oklahoma Press, 1987.

———. *Twenty Thousand Mornings: An Autobiography*. Norman: University of Oklahoma Press, 2014.

———. *Wah' Kon-Tah: The Osage and the White Man's Road*. Norman: University of Oklahoma Press, 1981.

Osage News. http://www.osagenews.org.

Rollings, Willard H. *The Osage: An Ethnohistorical Study of Hegemony on the Prairie-Plains*. Columbia: University of Missouri Press, 1995.

Skaggs, Jimmy M., ed. *Ranch and Range in Oklahoma*. Oklahoma City: Oklahoma Historical Society, 1978.

Tomer, John S., and Michael J. Brodhead, eds. *A Naturalist in Indian Territory: The Journals of S. W. Woodhouse, 1849–1850*. Norman: University of Oklahoma Press, 1996.

Wilson, Terry P. *The Osage*. New York: Chelsea House, 1988.

———. *The Underground Reservation: Osage Oil*. Lincoln: University of Nebraska Press, 1985.

Insects

Abbott, John C. *Dragonflies and Damselflies of Texas and the South-Central United States: Texas, Louisiana, Arkansas, Oklahoma, and New Mexico*. Princeton, N.J.: Princeton University Press, 2005.

———. *Dragonflies of Texas: A Field Guide*. Austin: University of Texas Press, 2005.

Capinera, John L., Ralph D. Scott, and Thomas J. Walker. *Field Guide to Grasshoppers, Katydids, and Crickets of the United States*. Ithaca, N.Y.: Cornell University Press, 2005.

Dole, John M., Walter B. Gerard, and John M. Nelson. *Butterflies of Oklahoma, Kansas, and North Texas*. Norman: University of Oklahoma Press, 2004.

Eaton, Eric R., and Kenn Kaufman. *Kaufman Field Guide to Insects of North America*. Boston: Houghton Mifflin, 2007.

Evans, Arthur V. *Beetles of Eastern North America*. Princeton, N.J.: Princeton University Press, 2014.

Heitzman, J. Richard, and Joan E. Heitzman. *Butterflies and Moths of Missouri*. Jefferson City: Missouri Department of Conservation, 2006.

Jackman, John A. *A Field Guide to Spiders and Scorpions of Texas*. Houston: Gulf Publishing, 1997.

Lockwood, Jeffery A. *Locust: The Devastating Rise and Mysterious Disappearance of the Insect That Shaped the American Frontier*. New York: Basic Books, 2004.

Lyons, Chuck. "1874: The Year of the Locust." *Wild West Magazine*, February 5, 2012. http://www.historynet.com/1874-the-year-of-the-locust.htm.

Monarch Watch. www.monarchwatch.org.

"Periodical Cicadas." Cicadas@www.magicicada.org.

Richardson, Patricia, and Dick Richardson. "Dung Beetles and Their Effects on Soil." *Ecological Restoration* 18 (Summer 2000): 116–117.

Schappert, Phil. *The Last Monarch Butterfly: Conserving the Monarch Butterfly in a Brave New World*. Buffalo, N.Y.: Firefly Books, 2004.

Smith, Charles. "Dung Beetles." *Noble Foundation Ag News and Views*, November 1, 1997. http://www.noble.org/ag/news-views/.

Thomas, Michelle. "Dung Beetle Benefits in the Pasture Ecosystem." *National Center for Appropriate Technology Weekly Harvest Newsletter*, 2001. https://attra.ncat.org/attra-pub/viewhtml.php?id=241.

U.S. Department of Agriculture. "Grasshoppers: Their Biology, Identification and Management." http://www.sidney.ars.usda.gov/grasshopper/.

Urquhart, Fred A. "Monarch Butterflies Found at Last: The Monarch's Winter Home." *National Geographic* 150 (August 1976): 160–173.

Reptiles, Amphibians, and Fish

Collins, Joseph T. *Amphibians and Reptiles in Kansas*. Lawrence: University of Kansas Natural History Museum, 1993.

Cross, Frank B., and Joseph T. Collins. *Fishes in Kansas*. Lawrence: University of Kansas Natural History Museum, 1995.

Ernst, Carl H., Jeffrey E. Lovich, and Roger W. Barbour. *Turtles of the United States and Canada*. Washington, D.C.: Smithsonian Institution Press, 1994.

Fitch, Henry S. *Autecology of the Copperhead*. Lawrence: University of Kansas Natural History Museum, 1965.

Hadley, Wayne F., and William A. Carter. "Fishes Known from Salt Creek, Osage County, Oklahoma." *Proceedings of the Oklahoma Academy of Science* 42 (1962): 128–132. http://digital.library.okstate.edu/oas/oas_pdf/v42/p128_132.pdf.

Johnson, Tom R. *Amphibians and Reptiles of Missouri*. Jefferson City: Missouri Department of Conservation, 2000.

Miller, Rudolph J., and Henry W. Robison. *Fishes of Oklahoma*. Stillwater: Oklahoma State University Press, 1973.

Pflieger, William L. *The Crayfishes of Missouri*. Jefferson City: Missouri Department of Conservation, 1996.

Stewart, Jeffrey G., Frances P. Gelwick, William J. Matthews, and Christopher M. Taylor. "An Annotated Checklist of the Fishes of the Tallgrass Prairie Preserve,

Osage County, Oklahoma." *Proceedings of the Oklahoma Academy of Science* 79 (1999): 13–17. http://digital.library.okstate.edu/oas/oas_pdf/v79/p13_17.pdf.